Jokes I Heard In Prison

by

Lt. Tom Hatchett

authorHOUSE®

AuthorHouse™
1663 Liberty Drive, Suite 200
Bloomington, IN 47403
www.authorhouse.com
Phone: 1-800-839-8640

First published by AuthorHouse 7/25/2008

ISBN: 978-1-4343-9904-5 (sc)

Printed in the United States of America
Bloomington, Indiana

This book is printed on acid-free paper.

PREFACE

About 20 years ago my Aunt Elizabeth and I got together and as always, we started telling jokes. I think most of the folks in my family looked forward to us getting together because between the two of us we usually kept every body laughing. At this time she told me I wish we had written all of these jokes down, we could have put them in a book and made a million dollars. I had just gotten into law enforcement, actually the prison system, and that is how Jokes I heard in Prison was started. I seriously doubt I'll make a million dollars, but if I can get a smile out of a bunch of people who read the book, then it will be a success. I started writing the jokes down and after all these years, what you have in your hands is my legacy.

Just imagine, the guy who hated English in High School actually getting a book published. That should be an inspiration to any High School English teacher!!

Well anyway for 23 years I swapped jokes with some of the most unlikely comedians you could ever expect to meet. I didn't just work in the prison system. I worked in several jails, juvenile detention homes, probation facilities and prisons across the state of Virginia. One common thread I found that seems to run in society is everybody loves a good laugh. We all want to be happy!! And nothing makes a person smile like a good joke, so I wholeheartedly hope you enjoy this book.

Two church members were going door to door, and knocked on Vickie's door who was not happy to see them. She told them in no uncertain terms that she did not want to hear their message, and slammed the door in their faces. To Vickies' surprise, however, the door did not close and, in fact, bounced back open. She tried again, really put her back into it, and slammed the door again with the same result the door bounced back open. Convinced these rude young people were sticking their foot in the door, she reared back to give it a slam that would teach them a lesson, when one of them said, "Ma'am, before you do that again you need to move your cat."

A young man excitedly tells his mother he's fallen in love and going to get married. He says, "Just for fun, Ma, I'm going to bring over 3 women and you try to guess which one I'm going to marry." The mother agrees. The next day, he brings three beautiful women into the house and sit them down on the couch. They all chat for a while. He then says, "Okay, Ma, guess which one I'm going to marry." She immediately replies, "The one in the middle." "That's amazing, Ma. You're right. How did you know?" asks the son. "I don't like her." says the mother.

In a hurry to get somewhere the lady was doing 75 in a 5mph zone. A State Patrol stopped her. He walked up to her car and asked, "Do you know why I pulled you over?" "Because you wanted to sell me tickets to the State Patrolmen's Ball?" she replied. "State Patrolmen don't have balls", he said…then realizing what he had just said…he let her go!

A young lady came home from a date, rather sad. She told her mother, "Jeff proposed to me an hour ago."

"Then why are you so sad?" her mother asked.

"Because he also told me he was an atheist. Mom, he doesn't even believe there's a hell."

Her mother replied, "Marry him anyway. Between the two of us, we'll show him how wrong he is."

A man was helping one of his cows give birth, when he noticed his 11-year-old son standing wide-eyed at the fence, soaking in the whole event.

The man thought, "Great…he's 11 and now I'm gonna have to start explaining the birds and bees. No need to jump the gun - I'll just let him ask, and I'll answer."

After everything was over, the man walked over to his son and said, "Well son, do you have any questions?"

"Just one Dad." gasped the still wide-eyed lad. Just as the father is preparing his birds and bees story, his son asks - "How fast was that calf going when he hit that cow?"

Southern Baptists John and Marie attended the same church. Marie went every Sunday and taught Sunday School. John went on Christmas and Easter and, once in a while, he went on one of the other Sundays. On one of those Sundays, he was in the pew right behind Marie and he noticed what a fine looking woman she was. While they were taking up the collection, John leaned forward and said, "Hey, Marie, how about you and me for dinner next Friday?" "Why Yes, John, that would be nice," said Marie. Well, John couldn't believe his luck. All week long he polished his car, and on Friday he picked up Marie and took her to the finest restaurant in town. When they sat down, John looked over at Marie said, "Would you like a cocktail before dinner?" "Oh, no, John," said Marie. "What would I tell my Sunday School class?" Well, John was setback a bit, so he didn't say much until after dinner. Then he reached in his pocket and pulled out a pack of cigarettes. He asked, "Would you like a smoke?" "Oh, no, John," said Marie. "What would I tell my Sunday School class?" Well, John felt pretty low after that, so he got in his car and was driving Marie home when they passed a Holiday Inn. He'd struck out twice already, so he figured he had nothing to lose. "Hey, Marie," said John, "how would you like to stop at this motel?" "Sure, that would be nice," said Marie. Well, John couldn't believe his luck. He did a U-turn right then and there and drove back to the motel and checked in with Marie. The next morning John got up first. He looked at Marie lying there in the bed. "What have I done? He shook Marie awake. "Marie, I've got to ask you one thing," said John. "What are you going to tell your Sunday School class?" Marie said, "The same thing I always tell them... "You don't have to smoke and drink to have a good time."

3

The Sunday School teacher asked, "Now, Johnny, tell me, Do you say prayers before eating?" "NO SIR," He replied, "We don't have to, my mom is a good cook!"

"Oh I sure am glad to see you" the little boy said to his Grandma on his mother's side. "now maybe Daddy will do that trick he keeps promising us" "What trick is that?" Grandma asked. I heard him tell mama he was going to climb the walls if you come to visit again."

I was standing on the corner,
causing no one harm,
When along came a policeman,
who took me by the arm.
We went around the corner,
and he rang a little bell,
a cruiser pulled up beside us
and took me straight to jail,
I woke the next morning
and looked upon the wall,
The roaches and the bedbugs
were playing a game of ball,
The score was 6 to 7,
the roaches were ahead,
The bedbugs kicked a field goal
that knocked me out of bed,
tobacco juice for coffee
and it was full of grounds
they fed us bread and butter,

th t weighed a half a pound,
so pass the word
an 1 tell everyone around,
sta y out of this hellhole,
ca se tyranny abounds
C use that's the way the treat you at Martinsville City
Ja l.

TEXAS CHILI

Fc those of you who have lived in Texas, you know how
tr e this is. They actually have a Chili cook-off about the
tir 1e the rodeo comes to town. It takes up a major portion
of he parking lot at the Astrodome. The notes are from an
in xperienced chili taster named Frank, who was visiting
Te as from the East Coast:

Frank: "Recently, I was honored to be selected as a
judge at a chili cook-off. The original person called in sick
at he last moment and I happened to be standing there at
th judge's table asking directions to the Budweiser truck,
wl en the call came in.

I was assured by the other two judges (Native Texans)
th t the chili wouldn't be all that spicy and, besides, they
to 1 me I could have free beer during the tasting, so I
ac epted."

Here are the scorecards from the event:

Chili # 1 Mike's Maniac Mobster Monster Chili

Judge # 1 -- A little too heavy on the tomato. Amusing kick.

Judge # 2 -- Nice, smooth tomato flavor. Very mild

Judge # 3 (Frank) -- Holy @#%$, what the hell is this stuff? You could remove dried paint from your driveway. Took me two beers to put the flames out. I hope that's the worst one. These Texans are crazy.

Chili # 2 Arthur's Afterburner Chili

Judge # 1 -- Smoky, with a hint of pork. Slight jalapeno tang.

Judge # 2 -- Exciting BBQ flavor, needs more peppers to be taken seriously.

Judge # 3 -- Keep this out of the reach of children. I'm not sure what I'm supposed to taste besides pain. I had to wave off two people who wanted to give me the Heimlich maneuver. They had to rush in more beer when they saw the look on my face.

Chili # 3 Fred's Famous Burn Down the Barn Chili

Judge # 1 -- Excellent firehouse chili. Great kick. Needs more beans.

Judge # 2 -- A beanless chili, a bit salty, good use of peppers.

Judge # 3 -- Call the EPA. I've located a uranium spill. My nose feels like I have been snorting Drano. Everyone knows the routine by now. Get me more beer before I ignite.

Barmaid pounded me on the back, now my backbone is in the front part of my chest. I'm getting @#%$-faced from all of the beer.

Chili # 4 Bubba's Black Magic

Judge # 1 -- Black bean chili with almost no spice. Disappointing.
Judge # 2 -- Hint of lime in the black beans. Good side dish for fish or other mild foods, not much of a chili.
Judge # 3 -- I felt something scraping across my tongue, but was unable to taste it. Is it possible to burn out tastebuds? Sally, the barmaid, was standing behind me with fresh refills. That 300-lb. bitch is starting to look HOT -- just like this nuclear waste I'm eating. Is chili an aphrodisiac?

Chili # 5 Linda's Legal Lip Remover

Judge # 1 -- Meaty, strong chili. Cayenne peppers freshly ground, adding considerable kick. Very impressive.
Judge # 2 -- Chili using shredded beef, could use more tomato. Must admit the cayenne peppers make a strong statement.
Judge # 3 -- My ears are ringing, sweat is pouring off my forehead and I can no longer focus my eyes. I farted and four people behind me needed the paramedics. The contestant seemed offended when I told her that her chili had given me brain damage. Sally saved my tongue from bleeding by pouring beer directly on it from the pitcher. I wonder if I'm burning my lips off. It really pisses me off

that the other judges asked me to stop screaming. Screw those rednecks.

Chili # 6 Vera's Very Vegetarian Variety

Judge # 1 -- Thin yet bold vegetarian variety chili. Good balance of spices and peppers.

Judge # 2 -- The best yet. Aggressive use of peppers, onions, and garlic. Superb.

Judge # 3 -- My intestines are now a straight pipe filled with gaseous, sulfuric flames. I @#%$ myself when I farted and I'm worried it will eat through the chair. No one seems inclined to stand behind me except that slut, Sally. She must be kinkier than I thought. Can't feel my lips anymore. I need to wipe my ass with a snow cone.

Chili # 7 Susan's Screaming Sensation Chili

Judge # 1 -- A mediocre chili with too much reliance on canned peppers.

Judge # 2 -- Ho hum, tastes as if the chef literally threw in a can of chili peppers at the last moment. I should take note that I am worried about Judge # 3. He appears to be in a bit of distress as he is cursing uncontrollably.

Judge # 3 -- You could put a grenade in my mouth, pull the pin, and I wouldn't feel a thing. I've lost sight in one eye, and the world sounds like it is made of rushing water. My shirt is covered with chili which slid unnoticed out of my mouth. My pants are full of lava-like @#%$ to match my shirt. At least during the autopsy, they'll know what killed me. I've decided to stop breathing, it's too painful. Screw it, I'm not getting any oxygen anyway. If I need air, I'll just suck it in through the 4-inch hole in my stomach.

Chili #8 Tommy's Toe-Nail Curling Chili

Judge # 1 -- The perfect ending, this is a nice blend chili. Not too bold but spicy enough to declare its existence.
Judge # 2 -- This final entry is a good, balance chili. Neither mild nor hot. Sorry to see that most of it was lost when Judge # 3 passed out, fell over and pulled the chili pot down on top of himself. Not sure if he's going to make it. Poor dude, wonder how he'd have reacted to really hot chili.

Mother: What seems to be the problem with you? You have been married three years and still no children. I had hopes of being a grandmother by now.

Daughter: I just don't know, Mom! Billy tries all the time, it's just that I have a lot of trouble swallowing.

A surgeon went to check on his blonde patient after an operation. She was awake, so he examined her.

"You'll be fine," he said.

She asked, "How long will it be before I am able to have a normal sex life again doctor?"

The surgeon seemed to pause, which alarmed the girl.

"What's the matter Doctor? I will be all right, won't I?"

He replied, "Yes, you'll be fine. It's just that no one has ever asked me that after having their tonsils out."

A blonde female police officer pulls over a blonde gal in a convertible sports car for speeding. She walks up to the car and asks the blond for her driver's license.

The blonde convertible driver searches through her purse in vain. Finally she asks, "What does it look like?"

The blonde police officer tells her, "It's that thing with your picture on it."

The blonde driver searches for a few more seconds, pulls out her compact, opens it and sure enough sees herself. She hands the compact to the blonde cop.

After a few seconds looking at the compact, the blonde cop rolls her eyes, hands the compact back to the blonde convertible driver and says, "If you would have told me you were a police officer when I first pulled you over we could have avoided this whole thing."

Sadie and Sophie are sitting at the kitchen table, bragging. "My daughter lives in a penthouse apartment in New York," says Sadie. "She goes out to dinner every night at a different restaurant, has beautiful furs and clothes, and lots of boyfriends. " Sophie replies, "Yeah, my daughter's a whore too."

A lawyer is standing in a long line at the box office. Suddenly, he feels a pair of hands kneading his shoulders, back, and neck. The lawyer turns around.

"What the hell do you think you're doing?"

"I'm a chiropractor, and I'm just keeping in practice while I'm waiting in line."

"Well, I'm a lawyer, but you don't see me screwing the guy in front of me, do you?"

As a young married couple, a husband and a wife lived in a cheap housing complex near the base where he was working. Their chief complaint was that the walls were paper-thin and that they had no privacy. This was painfully obvious when one morning the husband was upstairs and the wife was downstairs on the telephone. She was interrupted by the doorbell and went to greet her neighbor. "Give this to your husband," he said thrusting a roll of toilet paper into her hands. "He's been yelling for it for 15 minutes!"

A couple had been married for 45 years and had raised a brood of 11 children and were blessed with 22 grandchildren. When asked the secret for staying together all that time, the wife replies, "Many years ago we made a promise to each other: the first one to pack up and leave has to take all the kids...."

An atheist complained to a friend, "Christians have their special holidays, such as Christmas and Easter; and Jews celebrate their holidays, such as Passover and Yom Kippur; Muslims have their holidays. EVERY religion has its holidays. But we atheists," he said, "have no recognized national holidays. It's an unfair discrimination." His friend replied, "Well, why don't you celebrate April first?"

These young boys are sitting in the living room, watching TV with their parents. The mother looks over at the father with a wink and a nod toward the stairs to the bedroom. The father "gets" the message, and they both get up and head towards the stairs. The mother turns back to the 2 boys and says, "We're going upstairs for a minute. You two stay here and watch TV. We'll be right back, Ok?" The two boys nod OK, and the parents take off upstairs. The oldest of the two boys is old enough to know what's going on now, and he gets up and tiptoes upstairs. At the top of the stairs, he peeks into the room and shakes his head disapprovingly. Back downstairs he goes, back to his little brother. "Come with me," he says, and the 2 little boys tiptoe up the stairs. Halfway up, the older brother turns to the younger brother and says, "Now I want you to keep in mind, this is the same woman who used to bust our ass for sucking our thumb!!!!"

A wealthy man decided to go on a safari in Africa. He took his faithful pet dachshund along for company. One day, the dachshund starts chasing butterflies and before long the dachshund discovers that he is lost.

So, wandering about, he notices a leopard heading rapidly in his direction with the obvious intention of having lunch. The dachshund thinks, "OK, I'm in deep trouble now!"

Then he noticed some bones on the ground close by, and immediately settles down to chew on the bones with his back to the approaching cat. Just as the leopard is about to leap, the dachshund exclaims loudly, "Boy, that was one delicious leopard. I wonder if there are any more around here?"

Hearing this, the leopard halts his attack in mid-stride, as a look of terror comes over him, and slinks away into the trees. "Whew," says the leopard. "That was close. That dachshund nearly had me."

Meanwhile, a monkey who had been watching the whole scene from a nearby tree figures he can put this knowledge to good use and trade it for protection from the leopard. So, off he goes.

But the dachshund saw him heading after the leopard with great speed, and figured that something must be up. The monkey soon catches up with the leopard, spills the beans and strikes a deal for himself with the leopard.

The leopard is furious at being made a fool of and says, "Here, monkey, hop on my back and see what's going to happen to that conniving canine."

Now the dachshund sees the leopard coming with the monkey on his back, and thinks, "What am I going to do now?"

But instead of running, the dog sits down with his back to his attackers, pretending he hasn't seen them yet...and just when they get close enough to hear, the dachshund says, "Where's that monkey? I sent him off half an hour ago to bring me another leopard."

A married couple was on holiday in India. They were touring around the marketplace looking at the goods and such, when they passed this small sandal shop. From inside they heard a gentleman with an Indian accent say, "You foreigners! Come in. Come into my humble shop." So the married couple walked in. The Indian man said to them, "I have some special sandals I tink you would be interested in. Dey make you wild at sex like great desert camel." Well, the wife was really interested in buying the sandals after what the man claimed, but her husband felt he really didn't need them, being the sex god he was sure he was. The husband asked the man, "How could sandals make you into a sex freak?" The Indian man replied, "Just try dem on, Saiheeb." Well, the husband, after some badgering from his wife, finally gave in, and tried them on. As soon as he slipped them onto his feet, he got this wild look in his eyes, something his wife hadn't seen in many years! In the blink of an eye, the husband grabbed the Indian man, bent him violently over a table, yanked down his pants, ripped down his own pants, and grabbed a firm hold of the Indian's thighs. The Indian then began screaming, "WRONG FEET WRONG FEET!!

The Talking Dog

In Washington, D.C., a guy sees a sign in front of a house: "Talking Dog for Sale." He rings the bell and the owner tells him the dog is in the backyard. The guy goes into the backyard and sees a black mutt just sitting there. "You talk?" he asks. "Sure do." the dog replies. "So, what's your story?" The dog looks up and says, "Well, I discovered my gift of talking pretty young and I wanted to help the government, so I told the CIA about my gift, and in no time they had me jetting from country to country, sitting in rooms with spies and world leaders, because no one figured a dog would be eavesdropping. I was one of their most valuable spies eight years running." "The jetting around really tired me out, and I knew I wasn't getting any younger and I wanted to settle down. So I signed up for a job at the airport to do some undercover security work, mostly wandering near suspicious characters and listening in. I uncovered some incredible dealings there and I was awarded a batch of medals." "Had a wife, a mess of puppies, and now I'm just retired." The guy is amazed. He goes back in and asks the owner what he wants for the dog. The owner says, "Ten dollars." The guy says, "This dog is amazing. Why on earth are you selling him so cheap?" "Cause he's a liar. He didn't do any of that shit."

Q. How do you castrate a redneck?
A. You kick his sister in the jaw.
Q. Why does a dog lick his ass?

A. Because he knows that in five minutes, he'll be licking your face.

An escaped convict, imprisoned for 1st degree murder, had spent years of his life sentence in prison. While on the run, he broke into a house and tied up a young couple who had been sleeping in the bedroom. He tied the man to a chair on one side of the room and his wife on the bed. He got on the bed right over the woman, and it appeared that he was kissing her neck. Suddenly he got up and left the room. As soon as possible the husband made his way across the room to his bride, his chair in tow, and whispered, "Honey, this guy hasn't seen a woman in years. I saw him kissing on your neck and then he left in a hurry. Just cooperate and do anything he wants. If he wants to have sex with you, just go along with it and pretend you like it. Whatever you do don't fight him or make him mad. Our lives depend on it. Be strong and I love you." After spitting out the gag in her mouth, the half naked wife says: "Dear, I'm so relieved you feel that way. You're right, he hasn't seen a woman in years, but he wasn't kissing my neck... He was whispering in my ear. He said he thinks you're really cute and asked if we kept the Vaseline in the bathroom. Be strong and I love you, too."

A city cop was on his horse waiting to cross the street when a little girl on her new shiny bike stopped beside him.

"Nice bike," the cop said "did Santa bring it to you?"

"Yep," the little girl said, "he sure did!"

The cop looked the bike over and handed the girl a $5 ticket for a safety violation. The cop said, "Next year tell Santa to put a reflector light on the back of it." The young girl looked up at the cop and said, "Nice horse you got there sir, did Santa bring it to you?"

Yes, he sure did," chuckled the cop.

The little girl looked up at the cop and said, "Next year tell Santa the dick goes underneath the horse not on top."

Q What's the approximate Square Root of 69?
A: Eight Something

The Story of the Angel!

Not long ago and not far away Santa was getting ready for his annual trip....but there were problems everywhere... four of the elves got sick, and the trainee elves did not produce the toys as fast as the regular ones so Santa was beginning to feel the pressure of being behind schedule... then Mrs. Claus told Santa that her Mom was coming to visit...this stressed Santa even more ...when he went to harness the reindeer he found that three were about to give birth and two had jumped the fence and were out heaven knows where...more STRESS! And then, when he began to load the sleigh one of the boards on the sleigh cracked and the bag of toys fell to the ground and scattered all the toys...so being frustrated Santa went into the house for a cup of coffee and a shot of whiskey...but he found that the elves had hit the liquor cabinet and there was nothing there to drink...and in his frustration he dropped the coffee pot and it broke into hundreds of little pieces all over the kitchen floor...he went to get the broom and found that mice had eaten the straw that it was made from. Just then the doorbell rang and Santa cussed all the way to the door...he opened the door and there was a little angel with a great big Christmas tree.... And then the little angel said... "Santa where would you like to put this Christmas Tree"?? And that, my friend, is how the little angel came to be on top of the Christmas Tree...

When you're hospitalized, it pays to be nice to your nurse, even when you're feeling miserable. A bossy businessman learned the hard way after ordering his nurses around as if they were his employees. But the head nurse stood up to him. One morning she entered his room and announced, "I have to take your temperature." After complaining for several minutes, he finally settled down, crossed his arms and opened his mouth. "No, I'm sorry," the nurse said, "but for this reading, I can't use an oral thermometer." This started another round of complaining, but eventually he rolled over and bared his bottom. After feeling with her thermometer, the nurse the nurse announced, "I have to get something while this is registers. Now you stay just like that until I get back!" She left the door to his room open on her way out, and he cursed under his breath as he heard people walking past his door laughing. After almost an hour, the man's doctor came into the room. "What's going on here?" asked the doctor. Angrily, the man answers, "What's the matter, Doc? Haven't you ever seen someone having their temperature taken before?" "Yes," said the doctor. "But never with a daffodil."

Three men died and went to hell. When they get there the devil asks the first guy why he was there and he replied "I have a drinking problem." so the devil puts him in a room with every kind of alcohol he can imagine, then he locks the door. He then asks the 2nd guy why he was there the guy then says, "I can't stop cheating on my wife." The devil then puts him in a room with the hottest girl ever and locks the door. Then he asks the last guy why he was there he reply "I'm a pot smoker." So the devil locks him in a room with lots and lots of pot. In a hundred years the devil comes back and unlocks the first door and the guy comes out and says," I will never drink again! "So the devil sends him to heaven. He goes to the 2nd door and opens it and the guy comes out and says" I will never look at another woman again!" so the devil sends him to heaven. Finally he goes to the third door and opens it and goes in and there is the pot smoker sitting there with tears coming down his face. When devil asks him what is wrong he replies, Hey man you got a light?"

Who was the greatest inventor of all time? God was!... He took a rib from Adam and made a loudspeaker.

A man's car broke down as he was driving past a beautiful, old monastery. He walked up the drive and knocked on the front door of the monastery. A monk answered, listened to the man's story and graciously invited him to spend the night. The monks fed the man and led him to a tiny chamber in which to sleep. The man thanked the monks and slept serenely until he was awakened by a strange, beautiful sound. The next morning, as the monks repaired his car, he asked about the sound that woke him. The monks said, "We're sorry. We can't tell you about the sound. You're not a monk." The man was disappointed, but eager to be gone, so he thanked the monks for their kindness and went on his way. During quiet moments afterward, the man pondered the source of the alluring sound. Several years later, the man was driving in the same area. He stopped at the monastery on a whim and asked admittance. He explained to the monks that he had so enjoyed his previous stay, he wondered if he might be permitted to spend another night under their peaceful roof. The monks agreed and the man stayed. Late that night, he heard the sound again. The next morning, he begged the monks to explain the sound. The monks said, "We're sorry. We can't tell you about the sound. You're not a monk." By now, the man's curiosity had turned to obsession. He decided to give up everything and become a monk if that was the only way to learn about the sound. He informed the monks of his decision and began the long and arduous task of becoming a monk. Seventeen years later, the man was finally established as a true member of he order. When the celebration ended, he humbly went to the leader of the order and asked to be told the source of the sound. Silently the old monk led the new monk to a huge wooden door. He opened the door with a golden key. That door swung open to reveal a second door of silver, then a third of gold and so on until they had passed through twelve doors, each more magnificent than the last. The new monk's face was awash with tears of joy as he finally beheld the wondrous source of the mysterious sound he had heard so many years before.

But, I can't tell you what it was. You're not a monk.

A man is sitting at the bar in his local tavern, furiously imbibing shots of whiskey. One of his friends happens to come into the bar and sees him. "Lou," says the shocked friend, "what are you doing? I've known you for over fifteen years, and I've never seen you take a drink before. What's going on?" Without even taking his eyes off his newly filled shot glass, the man replies, "My wife just ran off with my best friend." He then throws back another shot of whisky in one gulp. "But," says the other man, "I'm your best friend!" The man turns to his friend, looks at him through bloodshot eyes, smiles, and then slurs, "Not anymore! He is!"

One evening during a poker game, a man was bragging to his friends about how his sister disguised herself as a man and was able to join the army.

"But, wait a minute," said one listener.

"Your sister will have to dress with the boys and shower with them, too.

Won't she?"

"Sure," replied the man.

"Well, won't they find out?" asked another poker player. The first man shrugged his shoulders and replied, "Sure, but who is gonna tell?"

A large, well established, lumber camp advertised that they were looking for a good lumberjack.

The very next day, a skinny little man showed up at the camp with his axe and knocked on the head lumberjack's door.

The head lumberjack took one look at the little man and told him to leave.

"Just give me a chance to show you what I can do," begged the skinny man. "Okay, see that giant redwood over there? Take your axe and go cut it down."

The skinny man headed for the tree, and five minutes later he returned to tell the head lumberjack that he had successfully cut the tree down.

The head lumberjack couldn't believe his eyes. "Where did you get the skill to chop down trees like that?" he asked the little man.

"In the Sahara Forest," replied the little man.

"You mean the Sahara Desert," said the lumberjack.

The little man grinned and replied, "Oh sure, that's what they call it now!

11 people were clinging precariously to a wildly swinging rope suspended from a crumbling outcropping on Mount Everest.

10 were blondes, one was a brunette.

As a group they decided that one of the party must let go. If that didn't happen the rope would break and everyone would perish.

For an agonizing few moments no one volunteered.

Finally, the brunette gave a truly touching speech saying she would sacrifice herself to save the lives of the others.

The blondes applauded.

When my husband worked at a prison, we only had one car so I used to roll out of bed at 5a.m. drive him to work, then come home and tumble back into bed and sleep.

One day while chatting with his colleagues he took out his wallet and showed them a photo of me.

"Wow!" a workmate remarked to my husband. "Who's that?"

"My wife," he replied proudly.

"Oh," his friend responded, looking puzzled. "Then who's that woman who drops you off."

Australian Police have been unable to recommend a prosecution for the following scam:

A company takes out a newspaper advertisement claiming to be able to supply imported hardcore pornographic videos. As their prices seem reasonable, people place orders and make payments via check.

After several weeks, the company writes back explaining that under the present law they are unable to supply the materials and do not wish to be prosecuted. So they return their customers' money in the form of a company check.

However, due to the name of the company, few people will present these checks to their banks. The name of the company: "The Anal Sex and Fetish Perversion Company."

A few stories from our nation's Emergency Rooms to prove that fact is stranger than fiction.

A 28-year old male was brought into the ER after an attempted suicide. The man had swallowed several nitroglycerin pills and a fifth of vodka. When asked about the bruises about his head and chest he said that they were from him ramming himself into the wall in an attempt to make the nitroglycerin explode.

A 50-year old woman came into the ER with a complaint of mild abdominal pain. During a pelvic exam the doctor found that the lady had inserted a whole chicken piece by piece into her private area. Unable to have children she was hoping that the chicken would turn into a baby.

A man in his mid-fifties did a Loreina Bobbit on himself in a drunken rage and ended up in the ER. The urologist thought that he could reattach the man's genitalia if it could be recovered and if it was in good condition. The police were dispatched to the man's house and the search was on. During the search, one of the officers heard a choking sound coming from the man's poodle that was sitting in the corner.

After a brief fight, the officer was able to retrieve the man's jewels from the dog's mouth. After inspection of the parts by the urologist it was decided that the man would need to be taught to pee while sitting. The officer was given a commendation from his precinct for medical assistance.

A woman with shortness of breath and who weighed approximately 500 lbs was dragged into the ER on a tarp by six firemen. While trying to undress the lady an asthma inhaler fell out of one of the folds under her arm. After an X-ray showed a round mass on the left side of her chest her massive left breast was lifted to find a shiny new dime. And last but not least during a pelvic exam a TV remote control was discovered in one of the folds of her crotch. She became known as "The Human Couch".

A doctor who spoke limited Spanish was rushed to a car in the ER parking lot to find a Spanish woman in the process of giving birth.

Wanting to tell the woman to push he started yelling "Puta! Puta! Puta!"

At this the grandmother started to cry and the baby's father had to be restrained. What the doctor should have been saying was "Puja!" (Push!).

Instead, he was saying, "Whore! Whore! Whore!"

An unconscious 36-year old male was brought to the ER with cocaine induced seizures. As a nurse pulled back his foreskin to insert a catheter a neatly folded twenty dollar bill fell out of the foreskin fold. When the man woke up and demanded to leave, the nurse gave him back his belongings and told him where she had found the money. His response: "It was a fifty!"

The most nonemergent ER visit: A male adolescent came in at 2 a.m. with a complaint of belly button lint.

A young female came to the ER with lower abdominal pain. During the exam and questioning, the female denied being sexually active. The doctor gave her a pregnancy test anyway and it came back positive.

The doctor went back to the young female's room.

Doctor: "The results of your pregnancy test came back positive.

Are you sure you're not sexually active?"

Patient: "Sexually active? No, sir, I just lay there."

Doctor: "I see. Well, do you know who the father is?"

Patient: "No. Who?"

A 92-year old woman had a full cardiac arrest at home and was rushed to the hospital. After about thirty minutes of unsuccessful resuscitation attempts, the old lady was pronounced dead. The doctor went to tell the lady's 78-year-old daughter that her mother didn't make it.

"Didn't make it? Where could they be?

She left in the ambulance forty-five minutes ago!"

A 15-year old boy was laying on a stretcher with his mother sitting next to him. The boy was coming down from "crank" (methamphetamine) that he had injected into his veins with needles he had been sharing with his friends. Concerned about this the doctor asked the boy if there was anything he might have been doing that put him at risk for AIDS. The boy thought for a while then said questioningly, "I've been screwing the dog?"

A 19-year old female was asked why she was in the ER. She said that she and her boyfriend were having sex and the condom came off and she wasn't able to retrieve it with her fingers. "Then I went to the bathroom and 'gagged' myself to vomit, but couldn't vomit it up either."

27

A slimy fellow proposed a one dollar bar bet to a full figured girl.

Despite her dress being buttoned to the neck, he could touch her breasts without touching her clothes.

Since this didn't seem remotely possible, she was intrigued and accepted the bet.

He stepped up, cupped his hands around her breasts and squeezed firmly.

With a baffled look, she said, "Hey, you touched my clothes" and he replied,

"Okay. Here's your a dollar."

Three men were sitting in a bar, one was French, one Itailan, and one American.

The Frenchman said "Last night I made love to my wife four times, and this morning she kept telling me how much she worshipped me."

So the Itailan said "Well, I had sex with my wife six times last night, and this morning she was too exhaused to speak."

The American remained silent, so the Frenchman smugly asks "So how many times did you have sex with your wife last night?"

"Once." the American replied.

"And what did she say this morning?" asked the Itailan.

"Don't stop!"

A truck driver was going south on I-75, when he came up on a weight station. When he pulled in and got on the scales to be weighed, the scale master told the driver that he was 900lbs. over weight. The truck driver replied, I can take care or that. The scale master asked he how could he fix the problem? The driver said, let me go around back, and I'll fix the overweight problem. The scale master agreed to let him fix his problem. About half an hour later the truck driver got back on the scales, and the scale master said, driver, you are still 900lbs. over weight. The truck driver said, I don't understand what went wrong. I let 50lbs. out of each tire on the rig. After thinking the problem over the scale master said, well 18 tires times 50lbs. would equal 900lbs. I guess my scales must be wrong. I'm sorry driver, you may continue on down the road, and have a nice day.

A Catholic priest, a Protestant minister, and a Jewish rabbi were discussing when life begins. "Life begins," said the priest, "at the moment of fertilization. That is when God instills the spark of life into the fetus." "We believe," said the minister, "that life begins at birth, because that is when the baby becomes an individual and is capable of making its own decisions and must learn about sin." "You've both got it wrong," said the rabbi. "Life begins when the children have graduated from college and moved out of the house!"

One day, an immigrant from Poland entered a New York City Police Precinct to report that his American wife was planning to kill him. The police officer on duty was intrigued by this and he asked, "How sure are ya that she is gonna kill ya? Did she threaten to kill ya?" "No," replied the nervous immigrant. "Did ya hear her tell someone else that she's gonna kill ya?" "No." "Did someone tell ya that your wife is gonna kill ya?" "No." "Then why in God's name did ya think she's gonna kill ya?" asked the exasperated police officer. "Because I found bottle on dresser and I think she gonna poison me!" He handed the police officer the suspect bottle. The police officer took one look at the label on the bottle and started to laugh out loud. The immigrant became indignant and said, "What so funny? Can't you see the label on bottle said, 'Polish Remover'?"

Wanda's dishwasher quit working so she called a repairman. Since she had to go to work the next day, she told the repairman, "I'll leave the key under the mat. Fix the dishwasher, leave the bill on the counter, and I'll mail you a check. Oh, by the way don't worry about my bulldog. He won't bother you. But, whatever you do, do NOT, under ANY circumstances, talk to my parrot!"

"I REPEAT, DO NOT TALK TO MY PARROT!!!"

When the repairman arrived at Wanda's apartment the following day, he discovered the biggest, meanest looking bulldog he has ever seen. But, just as she had said, the dog just lay there on the carpet watching the repairman go about his work.

The parrot, however, drove him nuts the whole time with his incessant yelling, cursing and name calling.

Finally the repairman couldn't contain himself any longer and yelled, "Shut up, you stupid ugly bird!" To which the parrot replied, "Get him, Spike!"

A blonde and her boyfriend were sitting at home one night and became bored. "Hey, let's play a game" she said. "What game?" was his bored reply. "Let's play hide'n'seek. I'll give you a blow-job if you can find me." "What if I can't find you?" "I'll be behind the piano."

A happily married person comes home from work, walks into the bedroom, and finds their partner screwing a stranger. He asks, "What the hell are you two doing?" Their partner turns to the stranger and says, "see what I mean? Didn't I tell you they was really stupid."

Early one morning, a mother went in to wake up her son. "Wake up, son. It's time to go to school!" "But why, Mom? I don't want to go." "Give me two reasons why you don't want to go." "Well, the kids hate me for one, and the teachers hate me, too!" "Oh, that's no reason not to go to school. Come on now and get ready." "Give me two reasons why I *should* go to school." "Well, for one,

31

you're 52 years old. And for another, you're the damn PRINCIPAL!"

Moods of a Woman

An angel of truth and a dream of fiction,
a woman is a bundle of contradiction,
she's afraid of a wasp, will scream at a mouse,
but will tackle her boyfriend alone in the house.
Sour as vinegar, sweet as a rose,
she'll kiss you one minute,
then turn up her nose,
she'll win you in rage, enchant you in silk,
she'll be stronger than brandy, milder than milk,
at times she'll be vengeful, merry and sad,
she'll hate you like poison,
and love you like mad.

Moods of a Man

Horny
Hungry
Thirsty
Sleepy

A college drama group presented a play in which one character would stand on a trapdoor and announce, "I descend into hell!" A stagehand below would then pull a rope, the trapdoor would open, and the character would plunge through. The play was well received. When the actor playing the part became ill, another actor who was quite overweight took his place. When the new actor announced, "I descend into hell!" the stagehand pulled the rope, and the actor began his plunge, but became hopelessly stuck. No amount of tugging on the rope could make him descend. One student in the balcony jumped up and yelled: "Hallelujah! Hell is full!"

The preacher spent his whole sermon relating the evils of sin and how all men are sinners with no exceptions. At the end of the sermon he asked rhetorically, "Now does anyone here think they are without sin?" He had only to wait a few seconds before a man in one of the back pews stood up. The pastor asked the man who had the audacity to stand after such a fiery sermon, "Sir, do you really think you are completely without sin?" The man quickly answered, "No sir, I'm not standing up for myself, but for my wife's first husband."

A man goes to the doctor's and says, "I would I like to get castrated". The doctor tries to convince him but the man won't listen. All he keeps on saying is, "I want to get castrated! I want to get castrated! I want to get castrated!" The doctor says; "your life will be changed after this operation. Do you still want to go ahead?" Man: "yes!"

After a few hours the man is walking in the hospital with a stick in his hand and legs apart he meets another man walking the same way. First man: "so even you got the operation done?" second man: "yeah after 37 years of my life I felt that it would be much better to get circumcised", first man: "Shit. That's the word!"

Wife to Husband: If I die, I want you to promise me, in the funeral procession, you'll let my mother ride in the first car with you.

Husband: All right, but it will ruin my day.

It's 2 in the morning and the travelling salesman calls the front desk at his motel and asks for some female company but with certain physical characteristics. "She's got to be taller than 6 ft. and weigh no more than 100 lbs.," he tells the desk clerk. 30 minutes later, there's a knock on his door and he opens it to see a tall, lithe young lady. "I'm here for your pleasure, sir," she says. "What do you weigh and how tall are you?" She replies, "6'2 and 97 lbs." "Perfect," he says. "Now take off all your clothes and get down on all fours on the floor." As she does this, he walks to the bathroom door, opens it and ushers in a big St. Bernard dog. The dog looks at the girl and the girl looks at the dog and the salesman says, "Now Fritz, do you see what you're going to look like if you don't finish your dinner?" (And WHAT were you thinking???)

There were two high school sweethearts who went out together for four years in high school and were both virgins and enjoyed losing their virginity with each other in 10th grade. When they graduated, they wanted to both go to the same college but the girl was accepted to a college on the east coast, and the guy went to the west coast.

They agreed to be faithful to each other and spend anytime they could together. As time went on, the guy would call the girl but she was never home and when he wrote, she would take weeks to return any letters. Even when he e-mailed her, she took days to return his messages. Finally, she confessed to him that she wanted to date around. He didn't take this very well and increased his calls and letters and e-mails trying to win back her love. Because she became annoyed, and now had a new boyfriend, she wanted to get him off her back. So what she did was this: She took a polaroid picture of her sucking her new boyfriend's unmentionables and sent it to her old boyfriend with a note reading, "I found a new boyfriend, leave me alone." Well needless to say, this guy was heartbroken, but even more so, he was pissed. So what he did next was awesome:

He wrote on the back of the photo the following: "Dear Mom and Dad, having a great time at college, please send more money!" and then mailed the picture to her parents.

The bride said she wanted three children, while the young husband said two would be enough for him. They discussed this discrepancy for a few minutes until the husband thought he'd put an end to things by saying boldly, "After our second child, I'll just have a vasectomy."

Without a moments hesitation, the bride retorted, "Well, I hope you'll love the third one just as if it's your own."

Our instructor was lecturing about self-examination of the breast or testicles when a female student asked another male student and me if we ever got an erection while we did self -examination of our testicles. We answered that it was possible that we had. You know, you don't really want everyone to know when you get aroused. She then asked, "What do you do about it?" We said in unison, "Nothing, why?" She then say, "You mean you go around with a hard penis all day?" We said no way! She then states, "You mean a man's penis will go down without having an orgasm?" We both said yes. At which time she says, "I'm going to kill my husband!"

Little Johnny was sitting in class one day and the teacher said: "Today we will learn multi-syllables. Does any one know any? Little Johnny stood up and said: "masturbate" wow said the teacher that's a mouth full. No miss Jones, you are thinking of a blow job!

The judge asked the defendant to please stand. "You are charged with murdering a teacher with a chain saw." From out in the gallery, a man shouts, "Lying bastard!" "Silence in the court!" the Judge says to the man who shouted. He turns to be defendant and says, "You are also charged with killing a paperboy with a shovel" "Damn

36

tightwad" the same man in the gallery blurted out "I said QUIET!" yelled the judge. To the defendant, "You are also charged with killing a mailman with an electric drill." "You jackass!" the man from the gallery yelled. The judge thundered at the man in the galley, "If you don't tell me right now the reasons for your outbursts I'll hold you in contempt!" The man answered back, "I've lived next door to that man for ten years now, but do you think he ever had a tool when I needed to borrow one?!"

Farmer Petrovich is whipping and slapping his sheep when the local minister comes walking around the corner. The minister says, "My, Farmer Petrovich, you're certainly giving that sheep a beating. You wouldn't do that to your wife, would you?" The farmer says, "I would if she farted and jumped sideways every time I tried to mount her!"

A guy stops to talk to a beautiful woman standing alone by a bus stop. "Hello, I must say, you are about the most beautiful woman I have ever met." "Thank you very much, replied the woman." The guy quickly follows up, "I was wondering if you'd sleep with me for a million dollars?" "A million dollars!" the girl responds. She slowly looks him up and down and then thinks for a moment and answers, "Yes, I would sleep with you for a million dollars." "How about five bucks? " responds the guy. "Five Bucks!, What kind of woman do you think I am?" "We've already determined that," he replies. "Now we're just haggling over money.

Larry, a local football star, is jogging down the street when he sees a building on fire. A lady is standing on a third story ledge holding her pet cat in her arms. "Hey, lady," yells Larry, "Throw me the cat." "No," she cries, "It's too far." "I play football, I can catch him." The smoke is pouring from the windows. Finally, the woman waves to Larry, kisses her cat goodbye, and tosses it down to the street. Larry keeps his eye on the cat as it comes hurtling down toward him. The feline bounces off an awning and Larry runs into the street to catch it. He jumps six feet into the air and makes a spectacular one handed catch. The crowd that has gathered to watch the fire breaks into cheers. Larry does a little dance, lifts the cat above his head, wiggles his knees back and forth, then spikes the cat into the pavement.

I have been where you fear to go...
I have seen what you fear to see...
I have done what you fear to do...
All these things I've done for you.

I am the one you lean upon...
The one you cast your scorn upon...
The one you bring your troubles to...
All these people I've been for you.

The one you ask to stand apart...
The one you feel should have no heart...

The one you call the man in blue...
But I am human just like you.

And through the years I've come to see...
That I'm not what you ask of me...
So take this badge and take this gun...
Will you take it? Will anyone?

And when you watch a person die...
And hear a battered baby cry...
Then so you think that you can be
All those things you ask of me...?

"Tears Of A Cop" - author unknown

An 80-year-old man is having his annual checkup. The doctor asks him how he's feeling. "I've never been better!" he replies. "I've got an 18-year-old bride who's pregnant and having my child! What do you think about that?" The doctor considers this for a moment, and then says, "Well, let me explain. I know a guy who's an avid hunter. He never misses a season. But one day he's in a bit of a hurry he accidentally grabs his umbrella instead of his gun and proceeds into the forest. As he walks into the woods suddenly a grizzly bear appears in front of him! He raises up his umbrella, points it at the bear, and squeezes the handle. The bear drops dead in front of him, suffering from a bullet wound in its chest. So what do you think about this story?" "That's impossible! Someone else must have shot that bear," the man said. "Exactly!" said the doctor.

No matter how legitimate my illness, I always sense my boss thinks I am lying. However, on one occasion, I had a valid reason, but lied anyway because the truth was too humiliating.

I simply mentioned that I had sustained a head injury and I hoped I would feel like coming in the next day. By then, I thought, I could think up a doozy to explain the bandage on my crown.

The accident occurred mainly because I conceded to my wife's wishes to adopt a cute little kitty. Initially, the new acquisition was no problem, but one morning I was taking my shower after breakfast when I heard my wife, Deb, call out to me from the kitchen.

"Ed!! The garbage disposal is dead. Come and reset it."

"You know where the button is," I protested through the shower (pitter-patter). "Reset it yourself!"

"I'm scared!" she pleaded. "What if it starts going and sucks me in?" (Pause) "C'mon, it'll only take you a second."

So out I came, dripping wet and buck naked, hoping to make a statement about how her cowardly behavior was not without consequence. I crouched down and stuck my head under the sink to find the button.

It is the last action I remember performing.

It struck without warning, without any respect to my circumstances. Nay, it wasn't a hexed disposal drawing me into its gnashing metal teeth. It was our new kitty, clawing playfully at the dangling objects she spied between my legs. She had been poised around the corner and stalked me as I took the bait under the sink. At precisely the second I was most vulnerable, she leapt at the toys I unwittingly offered and snagged them with her needle-like claws.

I lost all rational thought to control orderly bodily movements, while rising upwardly at a violent rate of speed, with the full weight of a kitten hanging from my masculine region. Wild animals are sometimes faced with a "fight or flight" syndrome. Men, in this predicament, choose only the "flight" option. Fleeing straight up, the sink and cabinet bluntly impeded my ascent; the impact knocked me out cold.

When I awoke, my wife and the paramedics stood over me. Having been fully briefed by my wife, the paramedics snorted as they tried to conduct their work while suppressing hysterical laughter.

At the office, my colleagues tried to coax an explanation out of me. I kept silent, claiming it was too painful to talk about.

"What's the matter, cat got your tongue?"

If they had only known

An old woman was taken to a gynecologist for the very first time, and of course the gynecologist was a very young and handsome fellow. The doctor was very thorough in his examination, and of course the old woman was quite embarrassed throughout the whole examination. Finally, the exam was over and the doctor told her to get dressed

41

and come in to his office to talk about his findings. The old woman listened intently as the doctor gave her the results. She then said she really only had one question for him. The doctor said, "What is the question you have?" "Tell me young man, does your mother know how you make a living?"

There was this couple that was married for 20 years and every time they had sex the husband always insisted on shutting off the lights. Well, after 20 years the wife felt this was stupid. She figured she would break him out of the crazy habit. So one night, while they were in the middle of doing it, she turned on the lights. She looked down and saw her husband was holding a dildo. She gets completely upset. "You impotent bastard," she screamed at him, "how could you be lying to me all of these years. You better explain yourself!" The husband looks her straight in the eyes and says, calmly, "I'll explain the dildo if you can explain our three kids.

Marty wakes up at home with a huge hangover. He forces himself to open his eyes, and the first thing he sees is a couple of aspirins and a glass of water on the side table. He sits down and sees his clothing in front of him, all clean and pressed.

Marty looks around the room and sees that it is in a perfect order, spotless, clean. So's the rest of the house. He takes the aspirins and notices a note on the table "Honey, breakfast is on the stove, I left early to go shopping. Love you."

So he goes to the kitchen and sure enough there is a hot breakfast and the morning newspaper. His son is also at the table, eating. Marty asks, "Son, what happened last night?"

His son says, "Well, you came home after 3 A.M., drunk and delirious. Broke some furniture, puked in the hallway, and gave yourself a black eye when you stumbled into the door."

Confused, Marty asks, "So, why is everything in order and so clean, and breakfast is on the table waiting for me?"

His son replies, "Oh that! Mom dragged you to the bedroom, and when she tried to take your pants off, you said, "Lady, leave me alone, I'm married'!"

A belligerent drunk walks into a bar and hollers: "I can lick any man in the place!" The nearest customer looks him up and down, then says: "Crude, but direct. Tell me, is this your first time in a gay bar?"

We blonds at the ofise are tired of all the the dum stoopid jokes about us. We think this is hairassment. It causes us grate stress and makes our roots turn dark. We have hired a loyer and he is talking to the loyers at Clairol. We will take this all the way to the supream cort if we have two. Ju Thomas knos all about hairassment and he will be on are side. We have also talked to the govner to make a new law to stop this pursicushun. We want a law that makes peepol tell brewnet jokes as much as blond jokes and every so often a red head joke. If we don't get our way we will not date anybody that ain't blond and we will make up jokes about you and we will laff.

Sined by the blonds at the ofise

A Texan, trying to impress a Bostonian with tales about the heroes of the Alamo, said, "I'll bet you never had anyone so brave around Boston." "Ever hear of Paul Revere?" asked the Bostonian. "Paul Revere?" said the Texan. "Isn't he the guy who ran for help?"

There was this West Va. sheriff and his deputy riding along the small town. They spot a car with out of town plates and decided to pull it over. The sheriff says "Where you from boy?" The man says Chicago. Sheriff says, "Don't lie to me son I saw them Illinois tags."

A man enters a restaurant and while sitting at his table, notices a gorgeous woman sitting at another table, alone. He calls the waiter over and asks for the most expensive bottle of champagne to be sent over to her, knowing that if she accepts it, she is his. The waiter gets the bottle and quickly sends it over to the girl, saying this is from the gentleman. She looks at the champagne and decides to send a note back over to the man. The note read: "For me to accept this bottle, you need to have a Mercedes in your garage, $1M in the bank, and 7 inches in your pants." Well, the man after reading this note, sends one of his own back to her and it read: "Just so you know -- I happen to have TWO Mercedes in my garage, I have over $2M in the bank, but not even for YOU, would I cut off 2 inches! Send the bottle back."

Start with a cage containing five monkeys. Inside the cage, hang a banana on a string and place a set of stairs under it. Before long, a monkey will go to the stairs and start to climb towards the banana. As soon as he touches the stairs, spray all of the other monkeys with cold water. After a while, another monkey makes an attempt with the same result - all the other monkeys are sprayed with cold water. Pretty soon, when another monkey tries to climb the stairs, the other monkeys will try to prevent it.

Now, put away the cold water. Remove one monkey from the cage and replace it with a new one. The new monkey sees the banana and wants to climb the stairs. To his surprise and horror, all of the other monkeys attack him. After another attempt and attack, he knows that if he tries to climb the stairs, he will be assaulted. Next, remove another of the original five monkeys and replace it with a new one. The newcomer goes to the stairs and is attacked. The previous newcomer takes part in the punishment with enthusiasm! Likewise, replace a third original monkey with a new one, then a fourth, then the fifth. Every time the newest monkey takes to the stairs, he is attacked. Most of the monkeys that are beating him have no idea why they were not permitted to climb the stairs or why they are participating in the beating of the newest monkey.

After replacing all the original monkeys, none of the remaining monkeys have ever been sprayed with cold water. Nevertheless, no monkey ever again approaches the stairs to try for the banana.

Why not?

Because as far as they know that's the way it's always been done around here. And that, my friends, is how company policy begins.

YOU KNOW YOU'RE TRAILER TRASH WHEN...

1. The Halloween pumpkin on your porch has more teeth than your spouse.

2. You let your twelve-year-old daughter smoke at the dinner table in front of her kids.

3. You've been married three times and still have the same in-laws.

4. You think a woman who is "out of your league" bowls on a different night.

5. Jack Daniels makes your list of "most admired people."

6. You wonder how service stations keep their restrooms so clean.

7. Anyone in your family ever died right after saying, "Hey y'all! Watch this!"

8. You think Dom Perignon is a Mafia leader.

9. Your wife's hairdo was once ruined by a ceiling fan.

10 Your junior prom had a daycare.

11 You think the last words of the Star Spangled Banner are, "Gentlemen start your engines."

12 You lit a match in the bathroom and your house exploded right off its wheels.

13 The bluebook value of your truck goes up/down, depending on how much gas is in it.

14 You have to go outside to get something from the fridge.

15 One of your kids was born on a pool table.

16 You need one more hole punched in your card to get a freebie at the House of Tattoos.

17 You can't get married to your sweetheart because there's a law against it.

18 You think loading a dishwasher means getting your .

Your toilet paper has page numbers on it.

20 Somebody hollers "Hoe Down" and your girlfriend hits the floor.

A nice young postal worker was sorting through the envelopes when she discovered a letter addressed as follows:

GOD
c/o Heaven

The letter enclosed told of how a little old lady, who had never asked for anything in her life, was desperately in need of $100 and was wondering if God could send her the money. The young lady was deeply touched and set up a collection from her fellow postal workers, collected $90, and sent it off to the old lady.

A few weeks later, another letter arrived addressed to God, so the young lady opened it.

It read, "Thank you for the money, God! I deeply appreciate it. However, I only received $90. Those creeps at the Post Office must have stolen $10."

A woman went into a store to buy her husband a pet for his birthday. After looking around, she found that all the pets were very expensive. She told the clerk she wanted to buy a pet, but she didn't want to spend a fortune.

"Well," said the clerk, "I have a very large bullfrog.

They say it's been trained to give blow jobs!"

"Blow jobs!" the woman replied. "It hasn't been proven but we've sold 30 of them this month" he said. The woman thought it would be a great gag gift, and what if it's true... no more blow jobs for her! She bought the frog.

When she explained froggy's ability to her husband, he was extremely skeptical and laughed it off.

The woman went to bed happy, thinking she may never need to perform this less than riveting act again.

In the middle of the night, she was awakened by the noise of pots and pans flying everywhere, making hellacious banging and crashing sounds.

She ran downstairs to the kitchen, only to find her husband and the frog reading cookbooks.

"What are you two doing at this hour?" she asked.

The husband replied, "If I can teach this frog to cook, your ass is history"

A high school English teacher reminds her class of tomorrow's final exam,

"Now class, I won't tolerate any excuses for you not being there tomorrow. I might consider a nuclear attack or a serious personal injury or illness, or a death in your immediate family - but that's it, NO other excuses whatsoever!"

A smart-ass guy in the back of the room raises his hand and asks, "What would you say if tomorrow I said I was suffering from complete and utter sexual exhaustion?" The entire class does its best to stifle their laughter and snickering. When silence is restored, the teacher smiles sympathetically at the student, shakes her head, and sweetly says, "Well, I guess you'd have to write the exam with your other hand."

It took 15 minutes for the class to come to order.

A man absolutely hated his wife's cat and decided to get rd of him one day by driving him 20 blocks from his home and leaving him at the park. As he was getting home, the cat was walking up the driveway. The next day he decided to drive the cat 40 blocks away. He put the beast out and headed home. Driving back up his driveway, there was the cat. He kept taking the cat further and further and the cat would always beat him home. At last he decided to drive a few miles away, turn right, then left, past the bridge, then right again and another right until he reached what he thought was a safe distance from his home and left the cat there.

Hours later the man calls home to his wife: "Jen, is the cat there?"

"Yes", the wife answers, "why do you ask?"

Frustrated, the man answered, "Put that son of a bitch on the phone, I'm lost and need directions!"

A woman and a baby were in the doctor's examining room, waiting for the doctor to come in for the baby's first exam. The doctor arrived, examined the baby, checked his weight, and being a little concerned, asked if the baby was breast-fed or bottle-fed. "Breast-fed" she replied.

"Well, strip down to your waist," the doctor ordered. She did. He pinched her nipples, then pressed, kneaded, and rubbed both breasts for a while in a detailed examination.

Motioning to her to get dressed, he said, "No wonder this baby is underweight. You don't have any milk."

"I know," she said, "I'm his Grandma, but I'm glad I came."

A man approached a very beautiful woman in the large supermarket and said, "I've lost my wife here in the supermarket.

Can you talk to me for a couple of minutes?"

The woman looked puzzled. "Why talk to me?" she asked.

"Because every time I talk to a woman with tits like yours, my wife appears out of nowhere"

23rd Psalm For The Workplace

The Lord is my real boss and I shall not want. He gives me peace, when chaos is all around me. He gently reminds me to pray before I speak and to do all things without murmuring and complaining.

He reminds me that He is my Source and not my job. He restores my sanity everyday and guides my decisions that I might honor Him in everything I do.

Even though I face absurd amounts of emails, system crashes, unrealistic deadlines, budget cutbacks, gossiping coworkers, discriminating supervisors and an aging body that doesn't cooperate every morning, I will not stop--for He is with me!

His presence, His peace, and His power will see me though. He raises me up, even when they fail to promote me. He claims me as His own, even when the company threatens to let me go.

His faithfulness and love are better than any bonus check. His retirement plan beats every 401K there is! When it's all said and done, I'll be working for Him a whole lot longer and for that, I bless His Name.

Q What do you call a lawyer with an I.Q. of 50?
A: Your honor.

Q: What do you call a lawyer who has gone bad?

A: Senator.

Q: How many lawyers does it take to roof a house?

A: Depends on how thin you slice them.

Q: What do you have when a lawyer is buried up to his neck in sand?

A: Not enough sand.

Q: When lawyers die, why are they buried in a hole 36 feet deep?

A: Because down deep, they are all nice guys!

Q: How do you stop a lawyer from drowning?

A: Shoot him before he hits the water.

Q: Have you heard about the lawyers word processor?

A: No matter what font you select, everything comes out in fine print.

Q: How many law professors does it take to change a light bulb?

A: You need 250 just to lobby for the research grant.

Q: Why did the post office recall the new lawyer stamps?

A: Because people could not tell which side to spit on.

A family took their frail, elderly mother to a nursing home and left her, hoping she would be well cared for. The next morning, the nurses bathed her, fed her a tasty breakfast, and set her in a chair at a window overlooking a lovely flower garden. She seemed okay, but after a while she slowly started to tilt sideways in her chair. Two attentive nurses immediately rushed up to catch her and straighten her up. Again she seemed okay, but after a while she slowly started to tilt over to her other side. The nurses rushed back and once more brought her back upright. This went on all morning. Later, the family arrived to see how the old woman was adjusting to her new home. "So Ma, how is it here? Are they treating you all right?" "It's pretty nice," she replied. "Except they won't let me fart."

When Billy was just a youngster, he went to the drugstore. He asked the pharmacist, "Sir, can you tell me where the ribbed condoms are?" The druggist replied, "Son, do you know what condoms are used for?" "Sure do. They keep you from getting venereal diseases." The druggist was impressed. "That's right, son. Do you know what the ribs are for?" Bill paused and then answered, "Well, not really, but they sure do make the hair on my goat's back stand up!"

Dear Abby:

I am a crack dealer in Jefferson County who has recently been diagnosed as a carrier of the HIV virus. My parents live in a suburb of Grubville and one of my sisters, who lives in High Ridge, is married to a transvestite. My father and mother have recently been arrested for growing and selling marijuana and are currently dependent on my other two sisters, who are prostitutes in Crystal City. I have two brothers. One is currently serving a non-parole life sentence in Fulton for murder of a teenage boy in 1994. The other brother is currently being held in the St Louis City Jail on charges of sexual misconduct with his three children. I have recently become engaged to marry a former Thai prostitute who lives in Arnold and is still a part time "working girl" in a brothel. Her time there is limited as we hope to open our own brothel with her as the working manager. I am hoping my two sisters would be interested in joining our team. Although I would prefer them not to prostitute themselves, it would get them off the street, and hopefully, the heroin habits. All things considered, my main problem is this. I love my fiance and look forward to bringing her into the family and I certainly want to be totally honest with her. Should I tell her about my distant cousin who is French? Signed, Worried About My Reputation

A man was walking along the street when he saw a ladder going into the clouds. As any of us would do, he climbed the ladder. He reached a cloud, upon which was sat a rather plump and homely looking woman. "Screw me or climb the ladder to success" she said. No contest, thought the man, so he climbed the ladder to the next cloud. On this cloud was a slightly thinner woman, who was slightly easier on the eye. "Screw me or climb the ladder to success" she said. "Well", thought the man, "might as well carry on. On the next cloud was an even more attractive lady who, this time, was really hot. "Screw me now or climb the ladder to success" she uttered. As he turned her down and went on up the ladder, the man thought to himself that this was getting better the further he went. On the next cloud was an absolute beauty. Slim, attractive, everything he could want. "Screw me or climb the ladder to success" she flirted. Unable to imagine what could be waiting, and being a gambling man, he decided to climb again. When he reached the next cloud, there was a 400 pound ugly man, arm pit hair showing, flies buzzing around his crotch. "Who are you?" the man asked. "Hello" said the ugly fat man said, "my name's Cass!"

An attractive lady is waiting in the emergency room. A doctor walks in to her room and asks her "What is the problem ma'am?" The lady replies, "Doctor, I have been having trouble with my asshole, it hurts really bad." The doctor tells the woman, "Why don't you lay on your stomach so I can take a look at it, OK?" So, the woman turns over and the doctor begins to examine her rear end. After a while, the doctor asks the young lady, "Ma'am, have you had anal sex lately?" The lady replies, "No, why?" The doctor then says, "Would you like to?"

At his wedding reception, the young groom's granddad congratulated his grandson and said: "The secret to enjoying a long and happy marriage, is to listen to each other at all times, respect each other's wishes and to try and have sex in moderation. That way, your marriage will last as long as your grandma's and mine has." Thanking him for his advice, the grandson said: "What's sex like then when you get older, granddad?" His granddad looked at his grandson, smiled and said: "Just like trying to play pool with a piece of rope!"

An American tourist in London found himself needing to take a leak something terrible. After a long search he just couldn't find any public bathroom to relieve himself. So he went down one of the side streets to take care of business. Just as he was unzipping, a London police officer showed up. "Look here, old chap, what are you doing?" the officer asked. "I'm sorry," the American replied, but I really gotta take a leak." "You can't do that here," the officer told him. "Look, follow me." The police officer led him to a beautiful garden with lots of grass, pretty flowers, and manicured hedges. "Here," said the policeman, "whiz away." The American tourist shrugged, turned, unzipped, and started pissing on the flowers. "Ahhh," he said in relief. Then turning toward the officer, he said, "This is very nice of you. Is this British courtesy?" "No," retorted the policeman. "It's the French Embassy."

A man was out, driving happily along in his car late one Saturday night. Before too long, a cop pulled him over. The policeman walked up to the man and asked, "Have you been drinking, sir?" "Why? Was I weaving all over the road?" "No," replied the policeman, "you were driving splendidly. It was the really ugly girl in the passenger seat that gave you away."

A little boy had a dog named Laddy. Billy and Laddy were the best of friends. Laddy would follow him to school and wait at the front gate of the house for Billy to come home. One day, Billy came home and walked in to find his mom at the kitchen table. "Billy," she said, "I have something to tell you. Laddy got hit by a car and he died." Billy just looked at her and said "Oh." He went up the stairs and came down a few moments later. "Where's Laddy mom?" He asked. "I just told you," said Billy's mom, "Laddy got hit by a car." Billy burst into tears and said "Laddy, I thought you said Daddy!"

Two old ladies were chatting one day and their subject finally got around to sex. The first old lady said she she enjoyed sex now just as much as ever. The second old lady was surprised and asked her what her secret was. The first old lady said when she hears her husband pulling the car into the garage she hurries and takes a shower, jumps into bed and throws her feet up over her head. When her husband comes into the bedroom, he gets turned on and has his way with her. The second old lady decides to try this approach. So that night when she heard her husband coming home, she takes a quick shower, jumps into bed and throws her feet up over her head. Her husband comes into the bedroom, takes one look and says, "For God's sake Maude, comb your hair and put your teeth in, you're starting to look like an ass!"

There was an attorney who got home late one evening after a very taxing day trying to get a stay of execution for a client, named Wilbur Wright, who was due to be hanged for murder at midnight. His last minute plea for clemency to the state governor had failed and he was feeling tired and depressed. As soon as he got through the door his wife started on about, "What time of night do you call this? Where the hell have you been?" and so on. Too shattered to play his usual role in this familiar ritual, he went and poured himself a very large whisky and headed off to the bathroom for a long hot soak -- pursued by the predictable sarcastic remarks. While he was in the bath the phone rang, which the wife answered to be told that her husband's client had been granted his stay of execution after all. Realizing what a day he must have had, she relented a little and went upstairs to give him the good news. As she opened the bathroom door she was greeted by the sight of her husband's rear view as he bent naked over the bath cleaning the tub. "They're not hanging Wright tonight," she said, at which the attorney whirled round and screamed hysterically, ..."For crying out loud . . .don't you ever stop bitching ?"

Two married buddies are out drinking one night when one turns to the other and says, "You know, I don't know what else to do. Whenever I go home after we've been out drinking, I turn the headlights off before get to the driveway. I shut off the engine and coast into the garage take my shoes off before I go into the house, I sneak up the Stairs, get undressed in the bathroom. I ease into bed and my wife STILL wakes up and yells at me for staying out so late!"

His buddy looks at him and says, Well, you're obviously taking the wrong approach. I screech into the driveway, slam the door, storm up the steps, throw my shoes in the closet, jump into bed, slap her on the ass and say, "WHO'S HORNY"?!!!"...and she acts like she's sound asleep.

A lady walks into a Furniture Store. She browses around, then spots the perfect leather sofa and walks over to inspect it. As she bends to feel the fine leather upholstery, a loud fart escapes her. Very embarrassed, she looks around nervously to see if anyone has noticed her little accident and hopes a sales person doesn't pop up right now. As she turns back, sure enough, there standing next to her is a salesman. "Good day, Madame. How may we help you today?" Very uncomfortably she asks, "Sir, what is the price of this lovely leather sofa?" He answers, "Madame, I'm very sorry to say that if you farted just touching it, you are going to shit when you hear the price."

When her late husband's will was read, a widow learned he had left the bulk of his fortune to another woman. Enraged, she rushed to change the inscription on her spouse's tombstone. "Sorry, lady," said the stonecutter. "I inscribed 'Rest in Peace' on your orders. I can't change it now." "Very well," she said grimly. "Just add, 'Until We Meet Again.' "

59

Toward the end of our senior year in high school, we were required to take a CPR course. The classes used the well-known mannequin victim, Resusci-Annie, to practice. Typical of most models, this Resusci-Annie was only a torso, to allow for storage in a carrying case. The class went off in groups to practice. As instructed, one of my classmates gently shook the doll and asked, "Are you all right?" He then put his ear over the mannequin's mouth to listen for breathing. Suddenly he turned to the instructor and exclaimed, "She said she can't feel her legs!"

Q: Men, how do you get a woman to argue with you?
A: Say something...

The District Attorney stared at the jury, unable to believe its verdict. Bitterly he asked, "What possible excuse could you have for acquitting this man?" The foreman answered, "Insanity." The D.A. said, "All twelve of you?"

During my brother's wedding, my mother managed to keep from crying---until she glanced at my grandparents. My grandmother had reached over to my grandfather's wheelchair and gently touched his hand. That was all it took to start my mother's tears flowing. After the wedding, Mom went over to my grandmother and told her how that tender gesture triggered her outburst. "Well, I'm sorry to ruin your moment," Grandmother replied, "but I was just checking to see if he'd fallen asleep."

An incompetent counterfeiter spent all day making his funny money. At the end of the day he realizes he spent all his time making $15 bills. He figures that the only way he's going to get anything from this batch of money is to find a place where the people aren't too bright and change his phony money for real cash. He travels to a small town in West Virginia and walks into a small "Mom and Pop" grocery store. He goes to the old man behind the counter and asks him, "Do you have change for a $15 bill?" The old man replies, "I sure do, Sonny. How would you like that? An 8 and a 7 or two 6's and a three?"

Bob was courting Mary. The young couple sat in the parlor of the girl's house night after night, much to the annoyance of Mary's father. One night he couldn't take any more. Standing at the top of the stairs, he yelled down, "What's that Bob fella doin' here all hours of the night?" "Why, Dad," said Mary, "Bob was just telling me everything that's in his heart!" "Well, next time," roared the father, "just let him tell you what's in his head, and it won't take half as long!"

A girl goes to the gynecologist for the first time. She's up in the stirrups, and the doctor notices she's trembling. He says: "You're nervous, aren't you?" "Yes, it's my first visit to a gynecologist." "Would you like me to numb you down there?" "Oh, yes please." He sticks his face between her legs and goes: "Num, num, num . . ."

Camilla had come to see Dr. Hardy. When the shrink began using sexual terms, she interrupted, "Wait, what is a phallic symbol?" "A phallic symbol," explained Hardy, "represents the phallus." "What's a phallus?" asked Camilla. "Well," said the analyst, "the best way to explain it is to show you." He stood up, unzipped his fly and took out his pecker. "This is a phallus." "Oh," said the girl. "It's like a prick, only smaller."

A minister and lawyer were chatting at a party: "What do you do if you make a mistake on a case?" the minister asked. "Try to fix it if it's big; ignore it if it's insignificant," replied the lawyer. "What do you do?" The minister replied "Oh, more or less the same. Let me give you an example. The other day I meant to say 'the devil is the father of liars,' but instead I said 'the devil is the father of lawyers,'... so I let it go...."

A wife invited some people to dinner. At the table, she turned to their six-year-old daughter and said, Would you like to say the blessing?" "I wouldn't know what to say," the girl replied. "Just say what you hear Mommy say," the wife answered. The daughter bowed her head and said, "Oh Lord, why in the Hell did I invite all these people to dinner?"

A man walks into a doctor's office and the doctor says to him, " I've got some good news and some bad news." "Tell me the good news first," the patient says. "The good news is that your penis is going to be two inches longer and an inch wider, "the doctor replies. "That's great!" says the patient." What's the bad news?" The doctor says, "It's malignant."

The poor country pastor was livid when he confronted his wife with the receipt for a $250 dress she had bought. "How could you do this!" he exclaimed. "I don't know," she wailed, "I was standing in the store looking at the dress. Then I found myself trying it on. It was like the Devil was whispering to me, 'Gee, you look great in that dress. You should buy it.'" "Well," the pastor persisted, "You know how to deal with him! Just tell him, "Get behind me, Satan!" "I did," replied his wife "and he said 'you look great from here too'."

Harley Davidson of the Harley Davidson Motorcycle Corporation, dies and goes to heaven. At the gates, an angel tells Davidson, "Well, you've been such a good guy and your motorcycles have changed the world. As a reward, you can hang out with anyone you want to in Heaven." Davidson thinks about it and says, "I wanna hang out with God, Himself." The befeathered fellow at the Gates takes Arthur to the Throne Room and introduces him to

God. Arthur then asks God, "Hey, aren't you the inventor of Woman?" God says, "Ah, yes." "Well," says Davidson, "You have some major design flaws in your invention: 1. there's too much front end protrusion 2. it chatters at high speeds 3. the rear end wobbles too much, and 4. the intake is placed too close to the exhaust." "Hmmm..." replies God, "hold on." God goes to the Celestial Supercomputer, types in a few keystrokes, and waits for the result. The computer prints out a slip of paper and God reads it. "It may be that my invention is flawed," God replies to Arthur Davidson, "but according to My Computer, more people are riding my invention than yours."

A man was wandering around a fairground and he happened to see a fortuneteller's tent. Thinking it would be good for a laugh, he went inside and sat down. "Ah....." said the woman as she gazed into her crystal ball. "I see you are the father of two children." "Hah, you fortune tellers are a sham," said the man scornfully. "I'm the father of *three* children." The woman grinned and said, "That's what *you* think..."

Little Johnny watched his Daddy's car pass by the school playground and go into the woods. Curious, he followed the car and saw Daddy and Aunt Jane in a passionate embrace. Little Johnny found this so exciting that he could not contain himself as he ran home and started to tell his mother.

"Mommy, I was at the playground and I saw Daddy's car go into the woods with Aunt Jane. I went back to look and he was giving Aunt Jane a big kiss, then he helped her take off her shirt. Then Aunt Jane helped Daddy take his pants off, then Aunt Jane........"

At this point Mommy cut him off and said, "Johnny, this is such an interesting story, suppose you save the rest of it for suppertime. I want to see the look on Daddy's face when you tell it tonight."

At the dinner table, Mommy asked little Johnny to tell his story. Johnny started his story about the car going into the woods, the undressing, Aunt Jane laying down on the back seat. Then Aunt Jane and Daddy started doing the same thing that Mommy and Uncle Bill used to do when Daddy was in the Army."

Sometimes you need to listen to the whole story before you interrupt!

A little old lady goes to see the minister of her church about a job as an organist. She is so poor and needs money desperately and the only thing she knows how to do is play the organ. She begged the minister to please give her a chance or she will be forced to live in the poor house.

The minister gave her his own sob tale. The church was in a major state of disrepair and they needed a lot of money to fix it up or the building inspectors will close them down soon and all the members of the church have not been doing much contribution towards renovating the church.

The organist made a deal with him, "If you allow me to play this Sunday for free, I guarantee you both, of our problems will be solved."

That Sunday in church, the little old lady played her heart out on the organ. Everyone sang out loudly to match her enthusiasm. As the congregation sat down, the minister asked the members to help restore the church.

"Any member who is going to commit to donating $500 or more today to the church repair fund, please stand up."

The organist then plays "The Star Spangled Banner". She was hired the next day:-)

A man and his wife were having a heated argument at breakfast. As he stormed out of the house, the man angrily yelled to his wife, "You aren't that good in bed either!" By midmorning, he decided he'd better make amends and phoned home. After many rings, his wife, clearly out of breath, answered the phone. "What took you so long to answer and why are you panting?" "I was in bed." "What in the world are you doing in bed at this hour?" "Getting a second opinion."

In the bookstore the other day, I saw a book entitled "Sex for Dummies". Why would someone want to teach dumb people how to reproduce?

Two couples had gone away for the weekend. The two guys, Jeff and Bill, have decided to try to persuade their wives to do a bit of partner swapping for the night. After several drinks that night they succeed. Jeff knows it's that time of the month for his wife and the thought of Bill not knowing this makes him smile. The guys agreed that when they sit around the breakfast table the following morning, they will tap their teaspoons on the side of their coffee mug the number of times that they did it with each other's wives. The next morning they are all at the breakfast table, slightly hung over and quite uncomfortable, when Jeff proudly taps his teaspoon three times against his coffee mug. After a brief moment of thinking, Bill takes his teaspoon and taps it once on the strawberry jam and three times on the peanut butter.

The prayer meeting was really jumping. The pastor asked for those who wanted to witness to get up and speak. A man stood and shouted, "I have lusted in my heart!" The pastor said, "Tell it all, Brother. Tell it all!" The brother said, "I have been a slave to the demon alcohol!" The pastor said, "Tell it all, Brother! Tell it all!" The brother said, "I have been unfaithful to my dear wife!" Again the pastor said, "Tell it all, Brother! Tell it all!" The brother said, "I have screwed a goat!" The pastor said, "I wouldn't have told that, Brother!"

Nick the Dragon Slayer had a long-standing obsession to nuzzle the beautiful Queen's voluptuous breasts, but he knew the penalty for this would be death. One day he revealed his secret desire to his colleague, Horatio the Physician, who was the King's chief doctor. Horatio the Physician exclaimed that he could arrange for Nick the Dragon Slayer to satisfy his desire, but it would cost him 1,000 gold coins to arrange it. Without pause, Nick the Dragon Slayer readily agreed to the scheme. The next day, Horatio the Physician made a batch of itching powder and poured a little bit into the Queen's brassiere while she bathed. Soon after she dressed, the itching commenced and grew intense.

Upon being summoned to the Royal Chambers to address this incident, Horatio the Physician informed the King and Queen that only a special saliva, if applied for four hours, would cure this type of itch, and that tests had shown that only the saliva of Nick the Dragon Slayer would work as the antidote to cure the itch. The King quickly summoned Nick the Dragon Slayer. Horatio the Physician then slipped Nick the Dragon Slayer the antidote for the itching powder, which he quickly put it into his mouth, and for the next four hours, Nick worked passionately on the Queen's voluptuous and magnificent breasts. The Queen's itching was eventually relieved, and Nick the Dragon Slayer left satisfied and touted as a hero. Upon returning to his chamber, Nick the Dragon Slayer found Horatio the Physician demanding his payment of 1,000 gold coins. With his obsession now satisfied, Nick the Dragon Slayer couldn't have cared less and, knowing that Horatio the Physician could never report this matter to the King, shooed him away with no payment made. The next day, Horatio the Physician slipped a massive dose of the same itching powder into the King's loincloth. The King immediately summoned Nick the Dragon Slayer...

The Moral of the Story: Pay your bills

There was a major sale at Victoria's Secret and John wanted to get Jill some really sexy lingerie. The store was packed with women for this big sale and before he knew it, John was pushed and shoved by frantic women all trying to get at the merchandise.

John remained calm for as long as he could, then bowed his head and pushed hard and effectively and plowed through the crowd of women.

"Hey you!" an angry female voice yelled out at him, "Try acting like a gentleman!"

"That's what I HAVE BEEN doing," John retorted, "But since that isn't working out for me, I'm gonna now act like you ladies!"

A drunk stumbles along a baptismal service on Sunday afternoon down by the river. He proceeds to walk down into the water and stand next to the Preacher. The minister turns and notices the old drunk and says, "Mister, Are you ready to find Jesus?" The drunk looks back and says, "Yes, Preacher, I sure am." The minister then dunks the fellow under the water and pulls him right back up. "Have you found Jesus?" the preacher asked. "Nooo, I didn't!" said the drunk. The preacher then dunks him under for quite a bit longer, brings him up and says, "Now, brother, have you found Jesus?" "Noooo, I did not Reverend." The preacher in disgust holds the man under for at least 30 seconds this time, brings him out of the water and says in a harsh tone, "My God, man, have you found Jesus yet?" The old drunk wipes his eyes and says to the preacher, "Are you sure this is where he fell in?"

Little Johnny and his father ran a one-mule farm and barely eked out a living. One day, Little Johnny hit the lottery, winning $50,000. He burned rubber into town, collected his money, and left more rubber all the way back home, where he told his father the good news and handed him a $50 bill. The father looked at the money for a moment and then said, "Little Johnny, you know I've always been careful with what little money we had. I didn't spend it on whiskey or women or frivolous things. In fact, I couldn't even afford a license to legally marry your Ma." "Pa!" Little Johnny exclaims, "do you know what that makes me?" "Sure do," said his father, fingering the fifty-dollar bill, "and a damn cheap one too!"

A farmer walked into a bar and saw the local tractor salesman sitting there, head hung low, obviously upset, drowning his sorrows in his beer. "What's up, John?" asked the farmer. "Gosh Bob, I'll tell you what ... if I don't sell a tractor soon, I'm gonna have to close my shop." "Now John, things could be worse," said Bob. "How do you figure?" asked John. "Well, John - you know my ornery cow, Bessie? I went to milk her this morning and she just kept flicking her tail in my face. So I grabbed a piece of rope and tied it up to the rafter. Then, the nasty thing went and kicked the bucket away! So I tied her leg to the wall. Then she kicked my stool right out from underneath me! But I was out of rope. So I took my belt off and used it to tie her other leg to the other side of the stall. Well wouldn't you just know it...my damn pants fell down." "And John, if you can convince my wife that I was in there to MILK that cow, I'll buy a tractor from you TODAY!"

During a jury selection process, the first lawyer began his questioning as an intimidating showman. He looked over the prospective jurors and asked, "Do any of you here today dislike lawyers?" Before the pause became too long, the judge said, "I do."

The pretty young lady was having a tooth pulled. The dentist gave her the usual "This won't hurt a bit" routine as he bent forward to begin. He immediately drew back in complete alarm. "Miss," he said in a barely audible whisper, "You have hold of my testicles!" "Yes, doc, I know," she smiled, "and we aren't going to hurt each other, are we?"

"Grandma, when you and Grandpa had your first baby, did Grandpa ever handle the middle-of-the-night feeding?" "No. I always did that." "That must have been before you had women's liberation." "No, it was before we had baby bottles."

A successful rancher died and left everything to his devoted wife. She was a very good looking woman, and determined to keep the ranch, but knew very little about ranching, so she decided to place an ad in the newspaper for a ranch hand.

Two men applied for the job. One was gay and the other a drunk. She thought long and hard about it, and when no one else applied, she decided to hire the gay guy, figuring it would be safer to have him around the house than the drunk.

He proved to be a hard worker who put in long hours every day and knew a lot about ranching. For weeks, the two of them worked, and the ranch was doing very well. Then one day, the rancher's widow said to the hired hand, "You have done a really good job and the ranch looks great. You should go into town and kick up your heels." The hired hand readily agreed and went into town one Saturday night. However, one o'clock came and he didn't return.

Two o'clock and no hired hand. He returned around two-thirty and found the rancher's widow sitting by the fireplace. She quietly called him over to her.

Unbutton my blouse and take it off," she said.

Trembling, he did as she directed.

"Now take off my boots."

He did so, slowly.

"Now take off my socks."

He did.

"Now take off my skirt."

He did.

"Now take off my bra."

Again with trembling hands he did as he was told.

Now," she said, "take off my panties."

He slowly pulled them down and off.

Then she looked at him and said, "If you ever wear my clothes to town again, I'll fire you on the spot."

A golfer was standing in the fairway, about 140 yards out, when a frog whispered from the rough, "Use an 8-iron." The golfer, deep in concentration pulled out his 8-iron and hit the shot. It rolled right into the cup for an eagle. "Now take me to Vegas," said the frog.

"What?" said the startled golfer, suddenly realizing it was a talking frog. "You heard me," repeated the frog, "take me to Vegas. I'm obviously a lucky frog, and we'll make a bundle!"

So the golfer picked up the frog and they flew to Vegas. In the casino, the frog whispered, "Go to the dice table and bet everything on the pass line." The shooter rolled a seven, and the man with the frog won $100,000.

Then the guy took the frog upstairs to his room and the frog said, "Kiss me." When he did, it turned into the most beautiful girl you've ever seen - deep brown eyes, blond hair, beautiful smile and 16 years old.

"And I swear, Your Honor, that's how she got in my room."

As I was nursing my baby, my cousin's six-year-old daughter came into the room. Never having seen anyone breast-feed before, she was full of questions. After mulling over my answers, she remarked, "My mom has some of those too, but the only one who gets to use them is Daddy"

A man was going to attend a Halloween party dressed in a costume of the devil. On his way it began to rain, so he darted into a church where a revival meeting was in progress. At the sight of his devil's costume, people began to scatter through the doors and windows. One lady got her coat sleeve caught on the arm of one of the seats and, as the man came closer, she pleaded, "Satan, I've been a member of this church for 20 years, but I've really been on your side the whole damn time."

Two guys are walking through the woods and come across this big deep hole. "Wow...that looks deep." "Sure does... toss a few pebbles in there and see how deep it is." They pick up a few pebbles and throw them in and wait... no noise "Jeeez. That is REALLY deep... here.. throw one of these great big rocks down there. Those should make a noise." They pick up a couple football-sized rocks and toss them into the hole and wait... and wait. Nothing. They look at each other in amazement. One gets a determined look on his face and says, "Hey...over here in the weeds, there's a railroad tie. Help me carry it over here. When we to is THAT sucker in, it's GOTTA make some noise." The two drag the heavy tie over to the hole and heave it in. Not a sound comes from the hole. Suddenly, out of the nearby woods, a goat appears, running like the wind. It rushes toward the two men, then right past them, running as fast as t's legs will carry it. Suddenly it leaps in the air and into the hole. The two men are astonished with what they've just seen... Then, out of the woods comes a farmer who spots the men and ambles over. "Hey... you two guys seen my goat out here?" "You bet we did! Craziest thing I ever seen! It came running like crazy and just jumped into this hole!" "Nah", says the farmer, "That couldn't have been My goat. My goat was chained to a railroad tie."

A woman went to the health clinic where she was seen by one of the new doctors, but after about 4 minutes in the examination room, she burst out of the office, screaming as she ran down the hall. An older doctor stopped her and asked what the problem was, and she told him her story. After listening, he had her sit down and relax in another room. The older doctor marched down hallway to the back where the first doctor was and demanded, "What's the matter with you? Mrs. Terry is 63 years old, she has four grown children and seven grandchildren, and you told her she was pregnant?" The new doctor continued to write on his clipboard and without looking up said, "Does she still have the hiccups?"

A guy calls his buddy the horse rancher and says he's sending a friend over to look at a horse. His buddy asks "How will I recognize him?" That's easy, he's a midget with a speech impediment". So, the midget shows up, and the

guy asks him if he's looking for a male or female horse. "A female horth."

So he shows him a prized filly. "Nith lookin horth. Can I thee her eyeth"?

So the guy picks up the midget and he gives the horse's eyes the once over.

Nith eyeth, can I thee her earzth"? So he picks the little fella up again, and shows him the horse's ears. "Nith earzth, can I see her mouf"? The rancher is gettin' pretty ticked off by this point, but he picks him up again and shows him the horse's mouth. "Nice mouf, can I see her twat"?

Totally mad as fire at this point, the rancher grabs him under his arms and rams the midget's head as far as he can up the horse's twat, pulls him out and slams him on the ground. The midget gets up, sputtering and coughing.

"Perhapth I should rephrase that; Can I thee her wun awound a widdlebit"?

There was a young man went to the doctor and said he wanted to get married but he was worried about the small size of his member. The doctor advised him to go and stay on a farm, dip his wick in milk several times a day, and have it sucked by a calf. Some months later when they met

76

in the street, the doctor said, "How's your marriage?" "Oh, I didn't get married doctor, I bought a calf instead."

Strange Feeling I've had this odd feeling for a little while. Not funny "ha-ha", but funny strange. It's a surrealistically subconscious feeling that I was abducted by aliens and thoroughly probed. Then a friend of mine told me they got me really drunk and dropped me off at a gay bar.

John and Mary were having dinner in a very fine restaurant. Their waitress, taking another order at a table a few paces away noticed that John was ever so slowly, silently sliding down his chair and under the table, while Mary acted quite unconcerned. Their waitress watched as John slid all the way down his chair and out of sight under the table. After the waitress finished taking the order, she came over to the table and said to the woman, "Pardon me, ma'am, but I think your husband just slid under the table." The woman calmly looked up at her and replied firmly, "Oh, no he didn't. In fact, my husband just walked in the front door."

Little Johnny was in the garden filling in a hole when his neighbor peered over the fence. Interested in what the cheeky-faced youngster was up to, he politely asked, "What are you up to there, Johnny?"

"My goldfish died," replied little Johnny tearfully, without looking up, "and I've just buried him."

The neighbor was concerned, "That's an awfully big hole for a goldfish, isn't it?"

Little Johnny patted down the last heap of earth then replied, "That's because he's inside your cat."

"Class I want everyone to go up to the chalk board and draw a picture of something exciting that happened over the summer.

"Mary gets up, draws a picture of an airplane, she's off to visit her grandmothers'.

Michael gets up draws a picture of his family on horse back, they're off into the wilderness for two weeks. Sharon gets up and draws a picture of a big skyscraper, she's on top waving hello to the world. Johnny picks up a piece of chalk, puts a dot on the board and sits down. Mrs. Johnson, "Johnny, what is that?" Johnny, "That's a period."

Mrs. Johnson, "What's so exciting about a period?"

Johnny, "Beats the hell out of me, but my sister missed one last month, and there sure was a lot of excitement around my house!"

A man was on his way home with a new car, which was absorbing all his attention, when it struck him that he had forgotten something. Twice he stopped, counted his parcels, searched his pockets, but finally decided he had everything with him. Yet the feeling persisted. When he reached home his daughter ran out, stopped short, and cried, "Daddy, where's Mommy?"

One night, an 87-year-old woman came home from Bingo to find her husband in bed with another woman.. She became violent and ended up pushing him off the balcony of their 20th-floor assisted-living apartment, killing him instantly. Brought before the court on the charge of murder, she was asked if she had anything to say in defense of herself. "Your Honor," she began coolly, "I figured that at 92, if he could fuck, he could fly."

Judge to convict: "The prisons are all full, so I'm sentencing you to five years in the waiting room at the department of motor vehicles."

During taxi, the crew of a US AIR departure flight to Ft. Lauderdale made a wrong turn and came nose to nose with a United 727. The irate ground controller (a female) screamed, "US Air 2771, where are you going? I told you to turn right on "Charlie" taxiway; you turned right on "Delta. Stop right there! I know it's difficult to tell the difference between C's & D's, but get it right!"

Continuing her lashing to the embarrassed crew, she was now shouting hysterically, "God, you've screwed everything up; it'll take forever to sort this out.

You stay right there and don't move until I tell you to! Then, I want you to go exactly where I tell you, when I tell you, and how I tell you. You got that, US Air 2771?"

The humbled crew responded, "Yes, Ma'am." The ground control frequency went terribly silent; no one wanted to engage the irate ground controller in her current state. Tension in every cockpit at LGA was running high. Then an unknown male pilot broke the silence and asked, "Wasn't I married to you once?"

After shopping at a busy store, another woman and I happened to leave at the same time, only to be faced with the daunting task of finding our cars in the crowded parking lot. Just then my car horn beeped, and I was able to locate my vehicle easily.

"Wow," the woman said. "I sure could use a gadget like that to help me find my car."

"Actually," I replied, "that's my husband."

A girl asks her boyfriend to come over Friday night and have dinner with her parents. This being a big event, the girl tells her boyfriend that after dinner, she would like to go out and "do it" for the first time.

Well, the boy is ecstatic, but he has never done it before, so he takes a trip to the pharmacist to get some protection. The pharmacist helps the boy for about an hour. He tells the boy everything there is to know about protection and doing it. At the register, the pharmacist asks the boy how many he'd like to buy; a 3-pack, a 10-pack, or a family pack. The boy insists on the family pack because he thinks he will be very busy, it being his first time and all.

That night, the boy shows up at the girl's parent's house and meets his girlfriend at the door. "Oh I'm so excited for you to meet my parents, come on in." The boy goes inside and is taken to the dinner table where the girl's parents are seated.

The boy quickly offers to say grace and bows his head. A minute passes, and the boy still deep in prayer with his head down. Ten minutes pass and still no movement from the boy. Finally, after 20 minutes with his head down, the girlfriend leans over and whispers to her boyfriend, "I had no idea you were so religious." The boy turns and whispers back, "I had no idea your father was a pharmacist."

A worried father telephoned his family doctor and said that he was afraid that his teenaged son had come down with V.D. "He says he hasn't had sex with anyone but the maid, so it has to be her."

"Don't worry so much," advised the doctor. "These things happen."

"I know, doctor," said the father, "but I have to admit that I've been sleeping with the maid also. I seem to have the same symptoms."

"That's unfortunate."

"Not only that, I think I've passed it to my wife."

"Oh God," said the doc, "That means we all have it."

A man walks into a bar one night. He goes up to the bar and asks for a beer. "Certainly, sir, that'll be 1 cent."

"ONE CENT!" exclaimed the guy and the barman replied "Yes."

So the guy glances over at the menu, and he asks "Could I have a nice juicy T-Bone steak, with chips, peas, and a fried egg?"

"Certainly sir, replies the bartender, but all that comes to real money."

"How much money?" inquires the guy.

"4 cents", he replies.

"FOUR cents!" exclaims the guy. "Where's the Guy who owns this place?"

The barman replies, "Upstairs with my wife."

The guy says, "What's he doing with your wife?"

The bartender replies, "Same as what I'm doing to his business."

These four gents go out to play golf one sunny morning. One is detained in the clubhouse, and the other three are discussing their children while walking to the first tee. 'My son,' says one, 'has made quite a name for himself in the homebuilding industry. He began as a carpenter, but now owns his own design and construction firm. He's so successful in fact, in the last year he was able to give a good friend a brand new home as a gift.'

The second man, not to be outdone, allows how his son began his career as a car salesman, but now owns a multi-line dealership. 'He's so successful, in fact, in the last six months he gave a friend two brand new cars as a gift.'

The third man's son has worked his way up through a stock brokerage and in the last few weeks has given a good friend a large stock portfolio as a gift.

As the fourth man arrives at the tee box, another tells him that they have been discussing their progeny and asks what line his son is in.

'To tell the truth, I'm not very pleased with how my son has turned out, he replies. 'For fifteen years, he's been a hairdresser, and I've just recently discovered he's a practicing homosexual. But, on the bright side, he must be good at what he does because his last three boyfriends have given him a brand new house, two cars, and a big pile of stock certificates.'

What Causes Arthritis?"

A drunk man who smelled like gin sat down on a subway seat next to a priest. The man's tie was stained, his face was plastered with red lipstick, and a half empty bottle of gin was sticking out of his torn coat pocket. He opened his newspaper and began reading. After a few minutes the man turned to the priest and asked," Say, Father, what causes arthritis?"

"My Son, it's caused by loose living, being with cheap, wicked women, too much alcohol and a contempt for your fellow man, sleeping around with prostitutes and lack of bath."

"Well, I'll be damned," the drunk muttered.

The priest, thinking about what he had said, nudged the man and apologized. "I'm very sorry. I didn't mean to come on so strong. How long have you had arthritis?"

"I don't have it, Father. I was just reading here that the Pope does...

A judge was interviewing a woman regarding her pending divorce, and asked, "What are the grounds for your divorce?"

She replied, "About four acres and a nice little home in the middle of the property with a stream running by."

"No," he said, "I mean what is the foundation of this case?"

"It is made of concrete, brick and mortar," she responded.

"I mean," he continued, "What are your relations like?"

"I have an aunt and uncle living here in town, and so do my husband's parents."

He said, "Do you have a real grudge?"

"No," she replied, "We have a two-car carport and have never really needed one." "Please," he tried again, "is there any infidelity in your marriage?"

"Yes, both my son and daughter have stereo sets. We don't necessarily like the music, but the answer to your questions is yes."

"Ma'am, does your husband ever beat you up?"

"Yes," she responded, "about twice a week he gets up earlier than I do."

Finally, in frustration, the judge asked, "Lady, why do you want a divorce?"

"Oh, I don't want a divorce," she replied. "I've never wanted a divorce. My husband does. He said he can't communicate with me!!

A boy comes home from school one day with a question on his mind, and goes to his father for an answer. "Father," he asks, "what is the difference between potentially and realistically?" His father is thoughtful for a moment, and then replies, "Well, I'll tell you what, son. Go and ask your mother if she'd sleep with the mailman for a million dollars."

The boy is confused, but follows his father instructions, and proceeds into the kitchen. When he returns, he tells father, "She said she would, Dad..." His father again looks thoughtful, and so the boy asks, "Now will you teach me the difference between potential and reality?'"

The father says, "I will, son, but first, go ask your sister if she'd sleep with the mailman for a million dollars." The boy is even more puzzled, but does as his father says. After he return from his sister's room, he says, "Yes, dad, she said she would sleep with the mailman for a million dollars. Now will you teach me the difference between potentially and realistically?"

The father looks up at his son, and says, "Alright son, think about this: Potentially, we've got two million dollars, but realistically - we're just living with a couple of sluts."

Mrs. Schmidlap hires a maid with beautiful blonde hair. The first morning, the girl pulls off the hair and says, "I wear a wig, because I was born totally hairless. Not a hair on my body, not even down there."

That night, Mrs. Schmidlap tells her husband. He says, "I've never seen anything like that. Please tomorrow, ask her to go into the bedroom and show you. I want to hide in the closet so I can have a look."

The next day, Mrs. Schmidlap asks the girl, the two of them go into the bedroom, and the girl strips and shows her. Then the girl says, "I've never seen one with hair on it. Can I see yours?"

So Mrs. Schmidlap pulls off her clothes and shows her. That night, Mrs. Schmidlap says to her husband, "I hope you're satisfied, because I was pretty embarrassed when that girl asked to see mine."

Her husband says, "You think you were embarrassed... I had the four guys I play poker with in the closet with me."

Little Johnny always did badly in math and his mother was very frustrated. She and her husband tried everything they could, flash cards, tutors, etc. However, they could never quite get him to understand math and study hard. As a last resort, his mother sent him to a Catholic school. When he came home from school, he ran straight up to his room and started studying. As she called him down for dinner, he ate quickly and ran up the stairs to study more.

After studying, he went straight to bed. This occurred for two months. Finally, one day Johnny brought her his report card. She looked at it and he had an A+ in math. Very surprised, she could not wait to ask him a question. "Johnny, what was it, what made you finally work so hard?" He looked at her and seriously answered, "Well, as soon as I walked in and saw the guy stuck on the plus sign, I knew they meant business."

An accountant gets home late one night and his wife says, "Where the hell have you been?"

He replies, "I was out getting a tattoo".

"A tattoo?" she frowned. "What kind of tattoo did you get?"

"I got a hundred dollar bill on my penis," he said proudly. "What the hell were you thinking?" she said, shaking her head in disdain. "Why on earth would an accountant get a hundred dollar bill on his penis?"

"Well, one, I like to watch my money grow," he began. "Two, once in a while, I like to play with my money...

Three, I like how money feels in my hand....

And lastly, instead of you going out shopping, you can stay right here at home and blow a hundred bucks anytime you want!

A young bride and groom to be had just selected the wedding ring. As the girl admired the plain platinum and diamond band, she suddenly looked concerned. "Tell me," she asked the elderly salesman, "is there anything special I'll have to do to take care of this ring?"

With a fatherly smile, the salesman said, "One of the best ways to protect a wedding ring is to dip it in dishwater three times a day."

A psychiatrist was conducting a group therapy session with four young mothers and their small children... You all have obsessions," he observed. To the first mother, Mary, he said, "You are obsessed with eating. You've even named your daughter Candy."

He turned to the second Mom, Ann: "Your obsession is with money. Again, it manifests itself in your child's name, Penny."

He turns to the third Mom, Joyce: "Your obsession is alcohol. This too manifests itself in your child's name, Brandy."

At this point, the fourth mother, Kathy, gets up, takes her little boy by the hand and whispers. "Come on, Dick, we're leaving."

Joe went to the Doctor because of severe recurring headaches. The doctor said, "Joe, the good news is I can cure your headaches...

The bad news is that it will require castration. You have a very rare condition, which causes your testicles to press up against the base of your spine, and the pressure creates one hell of a headache. The only way to relieve the pressure is to remove the testicles."

Joe was shocked and depressed. He wondered if he had anything to live for. He couldn't concentrate long enough to answer, but decided he had no choice, but to go under the knife. When he left the hospital he was without a headache for the first time in 20 years, but he felt like he was missing an important part of himself. As he walked down the street, he realized that he felt like a different person. He could make a new beginning and live a new life. He saw a men's clothing store and thought, "That's what I need a new suit." He entered the shop and told the salesman, "I'd like a new suit." The elderly tailor eyed him briefly and said, "Let's see ...size 44 long."

Joe laughed, "That's right, how did you know?" "Been in the business 60 years!"

Joe tried on the suit. It fit perfectly. As Joe admired himself in the mirror, the salesman asked, "How about a new shirt?" Joe thought for a moment and then said, "Sure." The salesman eyed Joe and said, "Let's see...34 sleeve and 16 and a half. Neck." Joe was surprised, "That's right, how did you know?" "Been in the business 60 years!"

Joe tried on the shirt, and it fit perfectly. As Joe adjusted the collar in the mirror, the salesman asked, "How about new shoes?" Joe was on a roll and said, "Sure."

The salesman eyed Joe's feet and said, "Let's see... 9- ½ E." Joe was astonished, "That's right, how did you know?" "Been in the business 60 years!" Joe tried on the shoes and they fit perfectly. Joe walked comfortably around the shop and the salesman asked, "How about some new underwear?" Joe thought for a second and said, "Sure." The salesman stepped back, eyed Joe's waist and said,

"Let's see...size 36." Joe laughed, "Ah ha! I got you! I've worn size 34 since I was 18 years old." The salesman shook his head, "You can't wear a size 34. A 34 underwear would press your testicles up against the base of your spine and give you one hell of a headache."

A big earth quake with the strength of 8.1 on the Richter scale has hit Mexico. 50,000 Mexicans have died and over a million are injured. The country is totally ruined and the government doesn't know where to start with providing help to rebuild. The rest of the world is in shock.

Canada is sending troopers to help the Mexican army control the riots. The European community is sending food and money. The United States is sending 150,000 replacement Mexicans.

A Doctor's Phone Rang at home at Three O'Clock in the morning. Sleepily he answered "Hello?" A very frantic woman said, "Doctor, our baby just swallowed a condom."

The Doctor said, "Take him to the Hospital, and I'll meet you just as soon as I get there."

He started putting on his clothes and was just getting ready to walk out the door, when the phone rang again. He answered "Hello?" A very calm voice on the other end of the line said, "That's all right Doctor, we found another one, never mind."

Q: How does an attorney sleep?
A: First he lies on one side, then he lies on the other.

Q: How many lawyer jokes are there?
A: Only three; the rest are true stories.

Q: How many lawyers does it take to change a light bulb?
A: You won't find a lawyer who can change a light bulb.
Now, if you're looking for a lawyer to screw a light bulb
. . .

Q: How many lawyers does it take to screw in a light bulb?
A: Three; one to climb the ladder, one to shake it, and one to sue the ladder company.

Q: What are lawyers good for?
A: They make used car salesmen look good.

Q: What do you call a lawyer gone bad?
A: Senator.

Q: What do you call a lawyer with an IQ of 50?
A: Your Honor.

Q: What do you get when you cross a bad politician with a crooked lawyer?

A: Chelsea.

Q: What do you throw to a drowning lawyer?
A: His partners or an anvil.

Q: What happens when you cross a pig with a lawyer?
A: Nothing; there are some things a pig won't do.

Q: What's the difference between a lawyer and a liar?
A: The pronunciation.

Q: What's the difference between a lawyer and an onion?
A: You cry when you cut up an onion.

Q: What's the difference between a lawyer and a vulture?
A: The lawyer gets frequent flyer miles.

Q: Why did God create snakes just before lawyers?
A: To practice.

Visiting a town in CA for campaigning, the presidential candidate checked into one of the posh hotel. Upon being shown to his room, he found a voluptuous young woman lying naked in the bed. Turning to the bellhop, he said, "What's the meaning of this? Are you trying to cause a scandal? I'm going to be the next president of the United States, and your establishment has the nerve to insult and offend me in this manner? I intend to sue the management for every penny it has!"

While the bellhop was quaking beneath the verbal attack, the sexy young girl quietly slid from the bed and began dressing. Noticing what she was doing, the candidate turned and said, "Hold on, young lady. No one's talking to you."

A nun and a priest were crossing the Sahara desert on a camel. On the third day out the camel suddenly dropped dead without warning. After dusting themselves off, the nun and the priest surveyed their situation. After a long period of silence, the priest spoke. "Well, sister, this looks pretty grim."

"I know, father."

"In fact, I don't think it likely that we can survive more than a day or two."

"I agree." "Sister, since we are unlikely to make it out of here alive, would you do something for me?"

"Anything father."

"I have never seen a woman's breasts and I was wondering if I might see yours."

"Well, under the circumstances I don't see that it would do any harm."

The nun opened her habit and the priest enjoyed the sight of her shapely breasts, commenting frequently on their beauty.

"Sister would you mind if I touched them?" She consented and he fondled them for several minutes.

"Father, could I ask something of you?"

"Yes, sister?"

"I have never seen a man's penis. Could I see yours?"

"I supposed that would be OK," the priest replied lifting his robe.

"Oh father, may I touch it?" The priest consented and after a few minutes of fondling he was sporting a huge erection.

"Sister, you know that if I insert my penis in the right place, it can give life."

"Is that true father?"

"Yes, it is, sister."

"Then why don't you stick it up that camel's ass and lets get the hell out of here."

The blond had been married about a year when one day she came running up to her husband jumping for joy. Not knowing how to react, the husband started jumping up and down along with her.

"Why are we so happy?" he asked.

"Honey, I have some really great news for you!" She said. "I'm pregnant!"

The husband was ecstatic as they had been trying for a while. Then she said "Oh, honey there's more."

"What do you mean more?", he asked.

"Well we are not having just one baby, we are going to have TWINS!"

Amazed at how she could know so soon after getting pregnant, he asked her how she knew.

"It was easy" she said, "I went to the pharmacy and bought the 2 pack home pregnancy test kit and both tests came out positive!"

Storming into the drugstore first thing Monday morning. The young man slammed a carton and a receipt down on the counter. "I came in here on Friday and purchased twelve dozen condoms," he yelled at the pharmacist. "Well, I counted them. There's only eleven dozen here." Looking at the man square in the eye, the pharmacist apologetically said, "So sorry, sir, to have ruined your weekend."

In a terrible accident at a railroad crossing, a train smashed into a car and pushed it down the tracks. Though no one was killed, the driver took the train company to court.

At the trial, the engineer insisted that he had given the driver ample warning by waving his lantern back and forth for nearly a minute. He even stood and convincingly demonstrated how he'd done it; the court believed his story, and the suit was dismissed. "Congratulations," the lawyer said to the engineer when it was over. "You did superbly under cross-examination." Thanks," he said, "but he sure had me worried." "How's that?" he lawyer asked. "I was afraid he was going to ask if the damned lantern was lit!"

A woman and a man are involved in a car accident; it's a bad one. Both of their cars are totally demolished but amazingly neither of them are hurt. After they crawl out of their cars, the woman says, "So you're a man.

That's interesting. I'm a woman. Wow, just look at our cars! There's nothing left, but we' re unhurt. This must be a sign from God that we should meet and be friends and live together in peace for the rest of our days." Flattered, the man replied, "Oh yes, I agree with you completely!

This must be a sign from God!" The woman continued, "And look at this, here's another miracle. My car is completely demolished but this bottle of wine didn't break. Surely God wants us to drink this wine and celebrate our good fortune." Then she hands the bottle to the man. The man nods his head in agreement, opens it and drinks half the bottle and then hands it back to the woman. She takes the bottle and immediately puts the cap back on, and hands it back to him. The man asks, "Aren't you having any?" The woman replies, "No, I think I'll just wait for the police."

MORAL OF THE STORY: Women are clever bitches. Don't mess with them.

A couple attending an art exhibition at the National Gallery were staring at a portrait that had them completely confused. The painting depicted three very black and totally naked men sitting on a park bench.

Two of the figures had black penises, but the one in the middle had a pink penis.

The curator of the gallery realized that they were having trouble interpreting the painting and offered his assessment. He went on for nearly half an hour explaining how it depicted the sexual emasculation of African-Americans in a predominately white, patriarchal society. "In fact," he pointed out, "some serious critics believe that the pink penis also reflects the cultural and sociological oppression experienced by gay men in contemporary society."

After the curator left, a young man in a West Virginia T-shirt approached the couple and said, "Would you like to know what the painting is really about?"

"Now, why would you claim to be more of an expert than the curator of the gallery?" asked the couple.

"Because I'm the guy who painted it," he replied. "In fact, there are no African-Americans depicted at all. They're just three West Virginia coal-miners, and the guy in the middle went home for lunch.

Discovering one of her students making faces at others on the playground, Ms. Levine stopped to gently scold the child. Smiling sweetly the teacher said, "Johnny, when I was a child, I was told if I made ugly faces I would stay like that."

Little Johnny looked up and replied, "Well you can't say you weren't warned...

"What am I supposed to do with this?" grumbled the motorist as the police clerk handed him a receipt for his speeding traffic fine.

"Keep it," the clerk advised. "When you get three of them, you get a bicycle."

An Irishman in a wheel chair entered a restaurant one afternoon and asked the waitress for a cup of coffee. The Irishman looked across the restaurant and asked, "Is that Jesus sitting over there?" The waitress nodded "yes," so the Irishman told her to give Jesus a cup of coffee on him.

The next patron to come in was an Englishman with a hunched back. He shuffled over to a booth, painfully sat down, and asked the waitress for a cup of hot tea. He also glanced across the restaurant and asked, "Is that Jesus over there?" The waitress nodded, so the Englishman said to give Jesus a cup of hot tea, my treat.

The third patron to come into the restaurant was a Redneck on crutches. He hobbled over to a booth, sat down and hollered, "Hey there, sweet thang, how's about gettin' me a cold glass of Coke!" He, too, looked across the restaurant and asked, "Is that God's boy over there?" The waitress nodded, so the Redneck said to give Jesus a cold glass of coke, and to put it on his tab.

As Jesus got up to leave, he passed by the Irishman, laid his hands on him, and said, "For your kindness, you are healed." The Irishman felt the strength come back into his legs, got up, and danced a jig out the door.

Jesus then passed by the Englishman, touched him, and said, "For your kindness, you are healed." The

Englishman felt the stiffness disappear from his back, and he jumped up, praised the Lord, and did a series of backflips out the door.

Then Jesus walked towards the Redneck. As Jesus extended his hands toward him, the Redneck shouted at Jesus, "Don't touch me...I'm drawin' disability!!!!!"

The Lone Ranger and Tonto went camping in the desert. After they got their tent all set up, they fell sound asleep. Some hours later, the Lone Ranger wakes his faithful friend and says, "Tonto, look up toward the sky and tell me what you see."

Tonto replies, "Me see millions of stars."

"What does that tell you?" asked The Lone Ranger.

Tonto ponders for a minute, then says, "Astronomically speaking, it tells me that there are millions of galaxies and potentially billions of planets. Astrologically, it tells me that Saturn is in Leo. Time wise, it appears to be approximately a quarter past three in the morning. Theologically, it's evident the Lord is all-powerful and we are small and insignificant. Meteorologically, it seems we will have a beautiful day tomorrow. What it tell you, Kemo Sabi?"

The Lone Ranger is silent for a moment, then says, "Tonto, you dumb ass, someone has stolen our tent."

A lady goes to the bar on a cruise ship and orders a Scotch with two drops of water. As the bartender gives her the drink she says, "I'm on this cruise to celebrate my 80th birthday and it's today."

The bartender says "Well, since it's your birthday, I'll buy you a drink."

As the woman finishes her drink, the woman to her right says, "I would like to buy you a drink, too."

The old woman says, Thank you. Bartender, I want a Scotch with two drops of water."

"Coming up," says the bartender.

As she finishes that drink, the man to her left says, "I would like to buy you one, too."

The old woman says, "Thank you. Bartender, I want another Scotch with two drops of water."

"Coming right up," the bartender says. As he gives her the drink he says, "Ma'am, I'm dying of curiosity.

Why the Scotch with only two drops of water?"

The old woman replies, "Sonny, when you're my age, you've learned how to hold your liquor. Water, however, is a whole other issue."

A woman goes to her lawyer to ask about getting a divorce.

The lawyer asks, "Does he beat you?"

"No, he does not."

"Does he keep you short of money?"

"No, he does not."

"Is he a perpetual drunkard?"

"No, he does not."

"Is he unfaithful to you?"

"Ahhh, we've got him there. He was not the father of my last child."

In the backwoods of Arkansas, a young redneck's wife went into labor in the middle of the night, and their elderly country doctor was called out to assist her in the delivery. Since there was no electricity, the doctor handed the father-to-be a lantern and said, "Here, you hold this high so's I can see what it is I'm doing." Soon, a baby boy was brought into the world. "Whoa there." said the doctor, "Don't be in a rush to put that lantern down... I think there's yet another one coming...."

Surely enough, in a few more minutes, the old doctor had delivered a baby girl. "No, no, don't be in a great hurry to be putting down that lantern. It seems there's yet another one in there!" cried the doctor in amazement. The bewildered redneck scratched his head and asked the country doctor, "Do you think it's the light that's attracting them?"

An overweight man was waiting in line at a bank.

There were two teenage boys in line behind him.

They were giggling and making fun of how fat the man was. After five minutes of this the man turned to the boys and asked them politely to stop, as he couldn't help his weight problem.

With this the boys asked: Oh, and why are you so fat Mister?

The Man turned around and replied: "Well, every time I screwed your mother, she gave me a cookie."

The instructor was demonstrating the wonders of static electricity to his class at MIT.

While holding a plastic rod in one hand and a wool cloth in the other, he told the class, "You can see that I get a large charge from rubbing my rod…"

That was pretty much the end of learning for that day.

THE CLASSIC FIVE KINDS OF SEX

1) The first is Smurf Sex. This happens during the honeymoon, you both keep doing it until you're blue in the face.

2) The second is Kitchen Sex. This is at the beginning of the marriage, you'll have sex anywhere, anytime, even in the kitchen.

3) The third kind is Bedroom Sex. You've calmed down a bit, perhaps have kids, so you gotta do it in the bedroom.

4) The fourth kind is Hallway Sex. This is where you pass each other in the hallway and say, "Fuck you!"

5) The fifth kind of sex: Courtroom Sex. This is when you get divorced and your wife screws you in front of everyone in the courtroom.

Women are like newspapers because...

* Older ones are not in demand near as much
* They're well worth looking over
* They have a great deal of influence
* You can't believe everything they say
* They always have the last word
* You should really get your own and not go
  borrowing your neighbor's

A mountain woman went to the doctor and was told to go home and come back in a couple of days with a specimen.

When she got home she asked her husband, "What is a specimen?" He replied, "Danged if I know. Go next door and ask Edith. She's a nurse"

The woman went next door and came back in about twenty minutes with her clothes all torn and with multiple cuts and bruises on her face and body.

What in the world happened? asked her husband.

Danged if I know," she replies. "I asked Edith what a specimen was and she told me to go piss in a bottle. I told her to go fart in a jug and then all hell broke loose."

A woman received a phone call that her daughter was very sick with a fever.

She left work and stopped by the pharmacy for some medication for her daughter. When returning to her car she found she had locked her keys inside. She had to get home to her sick daughter, and didn't know what to do.

She called her home to the baby sitter, and was told her daughter was getting worse. The babysitter said, "You might find a coat hanger and use that to open the door." The woman found an old rusty coat hanger on the ground, as if someone else had locked their keys in their car. Then she looked at the hanger and said, "I don't know how to use this."

She bowed her head and asked God for help.

An old rusty car pulled up, driven by a dirty, greasy, bearded man with a biker skull rag on his head. The woman thought, "Great God. This is what you sent to help me????" But she was desperate, and thankful.

The man got out of his car and asked if he could help.

She said, "Yes, my daughter is very sick. I must get home to her. Please, can you use this hanger to unlock my car?"

He said, "SURE." He walked over to the car and in seconds the car was opened.

She hugged the man and through her tears she said, THANK YOU SO MUCH....

You are a very nice man."

The man replied, "Lady, I ain't a nice man. I just got out of prison for car theft."

The woman hugged the man again and cried out loud....."THANK YOU GOD FOR SENDING ME A PROFESSIONAL!"

Little Johnny comes home with a note from the teacher and shows it to his mother. The note reads:

"Johnny is an intelligent little boy but spends too much time with girls."

The following day Johnny goes to school with a note from his mother to the teacher that reads,

"If you find a solution, please let me know. I have the same problem with his father."

Their once was a young woman who went to confession. Upon entering the confessional she said, "Forgive me Father, for I have sinned."

The priest said, "Confess your sins and be forgiven."

She said, "Last night my neighbor's husband made passionate love to me seven times."

The priest thought long and hard and then said, "Squeeze seven lemons into a glass and then drink the juice."

She asked, "Will this cleanse me of my sins?"

The Priest said "No, but it will wipe that damn smile off of your face!

Jill and John were invited to join friends at a quaint inn over an hour's drive away. Then Jill remembered that the last time she'd eaten there, her entree was tasteless, unevenly heated, and not well presented.

It was far from being a great dining experience.

When she explained why she didn't want to go, John was supportive. "You're right Jill, if we want a lousy meal, we don't have to drive so far," he said. "We can just stay here and you can cook."

Man Bashing!!

Q: What should you do if you see your ex-husband rolling around in pain on the ground?
A. Shoot him again.

Q: How can you tell when a man is well-hung?
A: When you can just barely slip your finger in between his neck and the noose.

Q: What do you call the useless piece of skin on the end of a man's penis?
A: His body.

Q: Why do little boys whine?
A: Because they're practicing to be men.

Q: How many men does it take to screw in a light bulb?
A: One - he just holds it up there and waits for the world to revolve around him.

Q: How many men does it take to screw in a light bulb?
A: Three - one to screw in the bulb, and two to listen to him brag about the screwing part.

Q: What do you call a handcuffed man?
A: Trustworthy.

Q: What does it mean when a man is in your bed gasping for breath and calling your name?
A: You didn't hold the pillow down long enough.

Q: Why do doctors slap babies butts right after they're born?
A: To knock the penises off the smart ones.

Q: Why do men name their penises?
A: Because they don't like the idea of having a stranger make 90% of their decisions.

Q: Why does it take 100,000,000 sperm to fertilize one egg?
A: Because not one will stop and ask directions.

Q: Why do female black widow spiders kill their males after mating?
A: To stop the snoring before it starts.

Q: What's the best way to kill a man?
A: Put a naked woman and a six-pack in front of him. Then tell him to pick only one.

Q: What do men and pantyhose have in common?
A: They either cling, run or don't fit right in the crotch!

Q: What is the difference between men and women...
A: A woman wants one man to satisfy her every need...A man wants every woman to satisfy his one need.

Q: How does a man keep his youth?
A: By giving her money, furs and diamonds.

Q: How do you keep your husband from reading your e-mail?
A: Rename the mail folder to "feminine issues"

A pompous minister was seated next to a cowboy on a flight to Oklahoma. After the plane was airborne, drink orders were taken. The cowboy asked for a whiskey and soda, which was brought and placed before him. The flight attendant then asked the minister if he would like a drink. He replied in disgust, "I'd rather be savagely raped by a brazen whore than let liquor touch my lips."

"The cowboy then handed his drink back to the attendant and said, "I didn't know we had a choice."

A gentleman was much surprised when the good-looking young lady greeted him by saying, "Good evening."

He could not remember ever having seen her before. She evidently realized that she had made a mistake, for she apologized, and explained. "Oh, I'm so sorry. When I first saw you I thought you were the father of one of my children."

She walked on while the man stared after her. The man thought for a moment and rushed back up to her. "I'm so sorry, but I have to ask, you aren't the girl I met at the party at Tom Hatchett's house and we had wild and wooly sex on the pool table are you." "NO" she said was a look of shock on her face, "I'm a schoolteacher and I thought you were little Jenny's father."

A man is walking past this house when a used condom comes flying out of the second story window and lands squarely on his head.

Rather disgusted and absolutely furious, he goes up to the front door and starts pounding on it. An elderly man opens it and asks him what caused him to knock so loudly. The passerby asks, "Who's in your upstairs room?"

The elderly man replies, "I can't see how it's any of your business. Since, you must know, my daughter and our intended son-in-law are upstairs."

The passerby hands him the used condom and says, "Well, I just wanted you to know that your intended grandchild just fell out of the window!"

A couple was dressed and ready to go out for the evening. They turned on a night light, turned on the answering machine on the phone line, covered their pet parakeet and put the cat in the backyard. They phoned the local cab company and requested a taxi. The taxi arrived and the couple opened the front door to leave their house.

The cat they had putout into the yard scoots back into the house.

They don't want the cat shut in the house because "she" always tries to eat the bird. The wife goes out to the taxi while the husband goes inside to get the cat. The cat runs upstairs, the man in hot pursuit.

The wife doesn't want the driver to know the house will be empty. She explains to the taxi driver that her husband will be out soon. "He's just going upstairs to say goodbye to my mother."

A few minutes later, the husband gets into the cab.

"Sorry I took so long," he says, as they drive away.

"Stupid bitch was hiding under the bed. Had to poke her with a coat hanger to get her to come out!

Then I had to wrap her in a blanket to keep her from scratching me. But it worked. I hauled her fat ass downstairs and threw her out into the back yard!"

The cabdriver hit a parked car…

Two women are fishing. Lisa always catches the most fish. Wanda asked her, "How do you do it? Every time we go fishing you always catch the most fish." Lisa replied, "When I wake up in the morning if my husbands thing is hanging off to the left, I fish off the left side of the boat. If his thing is hanging off to the right I fish off the right side of the boat." Wanda says, "What if his thing is standing straight up?" Lisa says, "Then you don't go fishing!"

A Sunday School teacher of preschoolers told her students that she wanted each of them to have learned one fact about Jesus by the next Sunday. The following week she asked each child in turn what he or she had learned.

Susie said, "He was born in a manger."

Bobby said, "He threw the money changers out of the temple."

Little Johnny said, "He has a red pickup truck, but he doesn't know how to drive it."

Curious, the teacher asked, "Where did you learn that, Johnny?"

"From my daddy," said Johnny. "Yesterday we were driving down the highway, and this red pickup truck pulled out in front of us and daddy yelled at him, 'Jesus Christ! Why don't you learn how to drive?'"

Two guys are drinking together at a bar and go into the bathroom. Standing at the latrine, Bill notices that his buddy is very well endowed.

"Wasn't always that way," the buddy says. "It's a transplant. I had it done over on Harley Street.

It cost a thousand bucks, but as you can see, it's well worth every cent."

So Bill visits the doctor on Harley Street that day. Six months later, the two guys meet up again at the bar. Bill explains, "I took your advice, but you were robbed. I got mine for $500, not a thousand."

They go back to the restroom to compare. "No wonder," his buddy says, "That's my old one!"

The doctor tells his patient: "Linda, I have some good news and some bad news."

Linda asks for the good news first.

"Well, the test results are in, and the good news is that you aren't suffering from Pre-menstrual Syndrome, as you'd feared."

"And the bad news?" Linda asks.

To which the Doc replies: "I'm afraid there's no cure for being a natural bitch."

Three Religious Truths

1. Jews do not recognize Jesus as the Messiah.

2. Protestants do not recognize the Pope as the leader of the Christian faith.

3. Baptists do not recognize each other in the liquor store or at Hooters.

Farmer John lived on a quiet rural highway. But, as time went by, the traffic slowly built up at an alarming rate. The traffic was so heavy and so fast that his chickens were being run over at a rate of three to six a day. So one day Farmer John called the sheriff's office and said, "You've got to do something about all of these people driving so fast and killing all of my chickens."

"What do you want me to do?" asked the sheriff.

"I don't care, just do something about those crazy drivers!"

So the next day he had the county workers go out and erected a sign that said:

SLOW: SCHOOL CROSSING

Three days later Farmer John called the sheriff and said, "You've got to do something about these drivers. The 'school crossing' sign seems to make them go even faster."

So, again, the sheriff sends out the county workers and they put up a new sign:

SLOW: CHILDREN AT PLAY

That really sped them up. So Farmer John called and called and called every day for three weeks. Finally, he asked the sheriff, "Your signs are doing no good. Can I put up my own sign?"

The sheriff told him, "Sure thing, put up your own sign." He was going to let the Farmer John do just about anything in order to get him to stop calling everyday to complain. The sheriff got no more calls from Farmer John. Three weeks later, curiosity got the best of the sheriff and he decided to give Farmer John a call. "How's the problem with those drivers. Did you put up your sign?"

"Oh, I sure did. And not one chicken has been killed since then. I've got to go. I'm very busy." He hung up the phone. The sheriff was really curious now and he thought to himself, "I'd better go out there and take a look at that sign... it might be something that WE could use to slow down drivers..."

So the sheriff drove out to Farmer John's house, and his jaw dropped the moment he saw the sign. It was spray-painted on a sheet of wood: NUDIST COLONY Go slow and watch out for the chicks.

A male-to-female transexual was being interviewed on a radio talk show. The DJ asked the transexual "What sort of pain did you experience during the operation?"

The transexual replied, "Well, when they cut my penis off, that really didn't hurt as much as I thought it would. Then they implanted the breasts in my chest, well, that really didn't hurt too much either..."

"Then you didn't experience any real physical pain at all then?"

"You're joking! What really hurt was when they removed half my brain and doubled the size of my mouth!"

Osama is worried about his future and calls Miss Cleo for advice. She said " Osama it does not look good at all you are going to die! Osama nervously asked, " When, When will I die?" Miss Cleo said, "It will be on an American holiday". "Which American holiday?" Miss Cleo said, "It does not matter. "When you die it will be an American holiday".

It was testimony night in the church. A lady got up and said, "We are living in a wicked land where sin is on every hand. I have had a terrible fight with the old devil all week."

Whereupon her husband, who was sitting glumly by her side said, "It's not all my fault either; she's tough to get along with."

As an obstetrician, I sometimes see unusual tattoos when working in labor and delivery. One patient had some type of fish tattoo on her abdomen. "That sure is a pretty whale," I commented.

With a smile, she replied, "It used to be a dolphin."

Recently a "Husband Shopping Center" opened in Houston, where women could go to choose a husband from among many men. It was laid out in five floors, with the men increasing in positive attributes as you ascended up the floors. The only rule was, once you opened the door to any floor, you must choose a man from that floor, and if you went up a floor, you couldn't go back down except to leave the place never to return. A couple of friends go to the place to find men. First floor, the door had a sign saying "These men have jobs and love kids."

The women read the sign and say, "Well, that's better than not having jobs, or not loving kids, but I wonder what's further up?" So up they go.

Second floor says "These men have high paying jobs, love kids, and are extremely good looking."

Hmmm, say the girls. But, I wonder what's further up?

Third floor: "These men have high paying jobs, are extremely good looking, love kids and help with the housework."

Wow! say the women. Very tempting, BUT, there's more further up! And up they go.

Fourth floor: "These men have high paying jobs, love kids, are extremely good looking, help with the housework, and have a strong romantic streak."

Oh, mercy me. But just think! What must be awaiting us further on!

So up to the fifth floor they go. The sign on that

door said, "This floor is empty and exists only to prove that women are impossible to please."

An irate woman burst into the baker's shop and said, "I sent my son in for two pounds of cookies this morning, but when I weighed them there was only one pound. I suggest that you check your scales."

The baker looked at her calmly for a moment or two and then replied, "Madam, I suggest you weigh your son."

"There are two million illiterates in America and everyday a vast majority of them give out directions at gas stations"

John walked into a Porsche dealership, opened the door a new Boxster, took a seat behind the wheel and smiled. A salesman approached and asked, "Are you thinking about buying this car?"

"Oh, I'm definitely going to buy this car," John said, "but I'm thinking about pussy."

A married couple were having a disagreement while sitting in bed. The wife said to her husband, "You're impossible."

To which the husband replied, "No. I'm next to impossible."

Research shows the first five minutes of life can be the most risky.

Somehow I think that the last five minutes aren't so hot either.

Tired from waiting for their overdue baby, my daughter and her husband broke the monotony one night with a trip to the movies. My daughter went inside to get seats while my son-in-law bought popcorn and drinks in the lobby.

Paying for the refreshments, my son-in-law knocked over his soda. The clerk mopped up the mess and refilled his cup. Rattled, he then joined his wife.

Talking over the background music, he dramatically described his embarrassing episode. One of his expressive gestures upset the bucket of popcorn. He sheepishly headed back to the lobby. When he was out of earshot, the woman sitting next to my daughter turned and said, "You're not going to let him hold the baby, are you?"

We were on our way to the hospital where our 16 year old daughter was scheduled to undergo a tonsillectomy. During the ride we talked about how the procedure would be performed.

"Dad," our teenager asked, "how are they going to keep my mouth open during the surgery?"

Without hesitation he quipped, "They're going to give you a phone."

A farmer goes out one day and buys a brand new stud rooster for his chicken coop. The new rooster struts over to the old rooster and says: "OK old fart, time for you to retire."

The old rooster replies, "Come on, surely you can't handle ALL of these chickens. Look what it has done to me. Can't you just let me have the two old hens over in the corner?"

The young rooster says, "Beat it! you are washed up and I am taking over."

The old rooster says, "I tell you what, young stud, I will race you around the farmhouse. Whoever wins gets the exclusive domain over the entire chicken coop."

The young rooster laughs, "You know you don't stand a chance old man, so to be fair I will give you a head start."

The old rooster takes off running. About 15 seconds later the young rooster takes off running after him.

They round the front porch of the farm house and the young rooster has closed the gap. He is already about 5 inches behind the old rooster and gaining fast. The farmer, meanwhile, is sitting in his usual spot on the front porch when he sees the roosters running by. He grabs his shotgun and...BOOM... He blows the young rooster to bits. The farmer sadly shakes his head and says, "Damn... third gay rooster I bought this month."

A couple just started their Lamaze class and they were given an activity requiring the husband to wear a bag of sand - to give him an idea of what it feels like to be pregnant. The husband stood up and shrugged saying, "This doesn't feel so bad."

The Lamaze teacher then dropped a pen and asked the husband to pick it up.

"You want me to pick up the pen as if I were pregnant, the way my wife would do it" the husband asked. "Exactly," replied the instructor.

To the delight of the other husbands, he turned to his wife and said, "Honey, pick up that pen for me."

One Sunday morning, while stationed at Osan Air Base in South Korea, I was in line for breakfast and noticed that the cook behind the counter looked kind of harassed. After I gave him my order, he asked me how I wanted my eggs. Not wanting to burden him further, I said cheerfully, "Oh, whatever is easiest for you." With that, he took two eggs, cracked them open onto my plate and handed it back to me.

You're in incredible shape," the doctor said. "How old are you again?"

"I am 78." The man said. "78?" asked the doctor. "How do you stay so healthy?

You look like a 60 year old." "Well, my wife and I made a pact when we got married that whenever she got mad she would go into the kitchen and cool off and I would go outside to settle down." the man explained. "What does that have to do with it?" asked the doctor. "I've pretty much lived an outdoor life."

A guy walks into a clinic to have his blood type taken. The nurse goes about taking the blood sample from his finger after finishing she looks around for a piece of cotton to wipe away the excess blood. She can't find it so she looks innocently at the guy and takes his finger and sucks it. The guy is so pleased he asks, "Do you think I could have a sperm count done?"

The next time your mind goes blank, do all of us a favor -- turn off the sound.

A businessman meets a beautiful girl and agrees to spend the afternoon with her for $500. So they do. Before he leaves, he tells her that he does not have any cash with him, but that he will have his secretary write a check and mail it to her, calling the payment 'RENT FOR APARTMENT. On the way to the office he regrets what he has done, realizing that the whole event was not worth the price. So he has his secretary send a check for $250 and enclosed the following typed note: "Dear Madam,

Enclosed find check in the amount of $250 for rent of your apartment. I am not sending the amount agreed upon, because when I rented the apartment, I was under the impression that: 1. it had never been occupied; 2. that there was plenty of heat; 3. that is was small enough to make me cozy.   However, I found out that it had been previously occupied, that there wasn't any heat, and that it was entirely too large."

Upon receipt of the note, the girl immediately returned the check for $250 with the following note:

"Dear Sir:

First of all, I cannot understand how you expect a beautiful apartment to remain unoccupied indefinitely. As for the heat, there is plenty of it, if you know how to turn it on. Regarding the space, the apartment is indeed of regular size, but if you don't have enough furniture to fill it, please do not blame the landlady. Send the rent in full or we will be forced to contact your present landlady!"

I heard about a lady who was speeding and an officer pulled her to the side of the road. She didn't have her seat belt on so as soon as she stopped, she quickly slipped it on before the officer got to her window. After talking to her about speeding, the officer said, "I see you are wearing your seat belt. Do you believe in wearing it at all times?"

"Yes, I do, officer," she replied.

"Well," asked the officer, "do you always do it up with it looped through the steering wheel"

An old married couple went to the doctor. The man saw the doc first and after the exam, the doc asked him if he had any concerns. The old man replied, "yes. Sometimes when I have sex with my wife, I get really hot and sweaty, and other times I am cold and shivering." well the doctor was puzzled and said, "well sir, I don't know what to tell you. You are perfectly healthy" so the old man left and it was the wife's turn, again the doctor reassured her she was fine and asked if she had any concerns. She said "no." In spite of the answer the doctor asked, "is your sex life doing alright?" she said, "yes everything is wonderful." The doc, even more puzzled, said, "well I was asking because when your husband was in here he said sometimes when the two of you have sex he gets really hot and other times he gets really cold." the old lady started laughing and said, "that old coot!!!!! We have sex twice a year. The first time is in July and the second time is in December!!!!!"

A lovely young Jewish girl was employed by a clothing firm in New York. She and her widowed mother shared the same ambition......her marriage to a wealthy man.

One day she returned from work, eyes red from crying. As soon as she entered the apartment she called, "MAMA, I'm pregnant! Don't get excited. The father is my boss."

She began to sob uncontrollably while her mother tried to console her. The next morning, the mother charged into the office of the boss. "YOU," she shouted, "What's its going to be?"

The elegantly attired man, handsome and unmarried and in his mid thirties, held up his hand: "Please take a seat, Mrs.Horowitz. I'm making all the arrangements. Your daughter Sherry will have the best doctor money can buy before the baby is born. She'll be in the best hospital. And afterward, I am arranging for a trust fund for her and the baby where she will receive a check for twenty five hundred dollars a week for life."

The mother was taken aback and thought for a moment. "Tell me," she said, "God forbid, Sherry should have a miscarriage, will you give her another chance?"

An attendant on a cross-country flight nervously announced: "I don't know how this happened, but we have 103 passengers aboard and only 40 dinners." When the passengers' muttering had died down, she continued, "Anyone who is kind enough to give up his meal so someone else can eat will receive free drinks for the length of the flight."

Her next announcement came an hour later. "If anyone wants to change his mind, we still have 29 dinners available!

Coming through the door after school one day, Little Johnny hollers out "Okay everyone in the house, please stand advised that I, Little Johnny have on this date made a complete fool of myself in sex-education class by repeating stories concerning storks as told to me by certain parties residing in this house!"

A couple are celebrating their fiftieth wedding anniversary-they go down to their old school-there, in a corner, they hold hands as they find their old desk where he had carved, "I love you, Sally."

On the way home, a bag of money falls out of the armored car in front of them. She picks it up and counts fifty thousand dollars. The husband says, "We've got to give it back." She says, "Finders keepers." And when they get home she hides it in the attic.

The next day, two FBI men show up at their home. They say, "Pardon me, did any one in this house find any money that fell out of an armored car yesterday?"

She says, "No."

The husband says, "My wife is lying, she took the money and hid it in the attic."

She says, "Don't believe him, he's a bit senile."

So they sit the man down and begin to question him. The FBI guy says, "Tell us the story from the beginning."

The old man says, "Well, my wife and I were on our way home from school..." The FBI guy looks at his partner and says, "Let's get the hell out of here."

A man telephones a law office and says: "I want to speak to my lawyer.

The receptionist replies: I'm sorry but he died last week.

The next day the same man phones again and asks the same question. The receptionist replies "I told you yesterday, he died last week."

The next day the man calls again and asks to speak to his lawyer. By this time the receptionist is getting a little annoyed and says "I keep telling you that your lawyer died last week. Why do you keep calling?"

The man says, "Because I just love hearing it."

Jill was trying to pull out of a parking place, and bashed the bumper of the parked car in front of her.

Witnessed by a handful of pedestrians waiting for a bus, she got out, inspected the damage, and proceeded to write a note to leave on the windshield of the car she had hit. The note read:

"Hello. I have just hit your car, and there are some people here watching me who think that I am writing this note to leave you my name and phone number. You should be so lucky!"

A cardiologist died and was given an elaborate funeral. A huge heart covered in flowers stood behind the casket during the service.

Following the eulogy, the heart opened, and the casket rolled inside. The heart then closed, sealing the doctor in the beautiful heart forever.

At that point, one of the mourners burst into laughter. When all eyes stared at him, he said, "I'm sorry, I was just thinking of my own funeral...I'm a gynecologist."

And at that point, the proctologist fainted.

One of the burdens of office of the small town mayor was his brother in-law, a fellow who liked to throw his or, rather, his in-law's political weight around.

The mayor had instructed his policemen and other city officials to treat him just like they would any other taxpayer.

The brother-in-law got a ticket for overtime parking.

He immediately descended in fury on police

headquarters, waving the ticket and sputtering, "Hey, do you know who I am?"

The desk sergeant surveyed him calmly, picked up his telephone and dialed the mayor's office. "Tell the mayor," he said to the secretary, "that his brother-in-law is down here and can't remember his name"

One day a gay man goes in for his doctor's appointment and asks the doctor, "Do you have anything to make hair grow on my chest?" The doctor immediately grabs a jar of vaseline and says," if you get a friend to rub this on your chest everyday, within a month or two you'll start to see some growth. The man replies," Well if that was true, I'd have a pony tail coming out my ass!"

One day, a diver was enjoying the aquatic world 20 feet below sea level. He noticed a guy at the same depth, but with no scuba gear whatsoever. The diver went below another 20 feet, and the guy joined him a few minutes later. The diver went down 25 feet more, and minutes later, the same guy joined him.

This confused the diver, so he took out a waterproof chalkboard set, and wrote, "How the heck are you able to stay under this deep without equipment?"

The guy took the board and chalk, erased what the diver had written, and wrote, ..."I'm drowning, you fucking moron...!"

There were these three homosexuals at a crematory grieving over their loved ones. The first one says to the others, "I'm going to spread my lover's ashes over the hill we used to lay and watch the sunset. It was sooo beautiful." The other homo says, "I'm going to spread my lover's ashes over the garden we used to have. We would always smell the roses."

127

The third one says, "I'm going to mix my lover's ashes into a bowl of chili and eat him." The other two look at him in disgusting and say what a horrible lover he is. He replies, " I just want to feel him tear the hell out of my a.. one more time!"

The Pope had just finished a tour of the East Coast and was taking a limousine to the airport. Having never driven a limo, he asked the chauffeur if he could drive for a while. Without much of a choice, the chauffeur climbed in the back of the limo and the Pope took the wheel.

After gleefully accelerating to about 90 mph, the Pope was pulled over by the State Patrol. The trooper came to his window, took a look inside, and said, "Just a moment, please. I need to call in."

The trooper called in and asked for the chief. He told the chief, "I've got a REALLY important person pulled over and I need to know what to do."

The chief replied, "Who is it? A senator?"

The trooper said, "No, even more important."

The chief asked, "It's the Governor, isn't it?"

"No. More important."

"The President?"

"No. More important."

"Well, Who the heck is it?!," screams the chief.

"I don't know," said the trooper. "But he's got the Pope as a chauffeur."

Two old women were sitting on a bench waiting for their bus. The buses were running late, and a lot of time passed. Finally, one woman turned to the other and said, "You know, I've been sitting here so long, my butt fell asleep!"

"I know," the other woman replied. "I heard it snoring...!"

The teacher in Johnny's school asked the class what their parents did for a living. One little girl said her father was a doctor, another said her mother was an engineer. When it was Little Johnny's turn, he stood up and said "My mom's a whore!"

Naturally, after that remark, he got sent off to the principal's office. Then, 15 minutes later, he returned. So the teacher asked "Did you tell the principal what you said in class?"

Johnny said, "Yes."

"Well, what did the principal say?"

"He said that every job is important in our economy, gave me an apple and asked for my phone number!"

Sunday school teacher was teaching her class about the difference between right and wrong.

"All right children, let's take another example," she said. "If I were to get into a man's pocket and take his billfold with all his money, what would I be?"

Little Johnny raises his hand, and with a confident smile, he blurts out, "you'd be his wife!"

When it was finally her turn to take care of the elderly Father Joe, the novice Joan was taken aside by the mother superior. "I must warn you," she said, "that although Father Joe is old in body, he is young at heart. It is important that when you give him his bath, you never look below his waist. Other wise, he will become very excited."

With that, Joan went to look after the aged priest. Shortly after in a big sob, Joan hunted out the mother superior. "Forgive me," the novice said, "but when I was bathing father Joe, I - I looked down, and as you said, he became aroused." "And what happened?" "I - I lay with him. He said that I would surely go to heaven if I let him put his key to the gates of St. Peter in my lock." "Why, that old bastard!" The mother superior fumed. "For years, he has been telling me it's Gabriel's trumpet!"

An American submarine was patrolling the water border when a radio when off the crew fixed it and waited for the transmission to come back when it did the crew heard "This is the Canadians Change your course to avoid collision" The Americans replied "No, You change your course to avoid collision!" the Canadians reply "No, you don't-" and were cut off by the Americans who said " This is the command ship of the American fleet. We are armed with torpedoes nukes and destroyers. This is the most powerful vessel on the face of the earth. Now will YOU change your course" then there was silence the

Canadians replied "This is the Canadian Lighthouse It's Your Call!"

A young lady whom thought she was overweight went to see a dietitian. She walked into his office and asked several questions about dieting, exercise, and other things. Her final question to the dietitian sparked interest in him. She asked, "How many calories are in sperm?"

"Why?" he replied.

She explained some of the things she liked to do. After thinking a minute he said, "I really have no clue, but if you are consuming that much of it, then no guy is going to care if you are a little chunky!"

The other night I was invited out for a night with "the girls." I told my husband that I would be home by midnight. "I promise!"

Well, the hours passed and the margaritas went down way too easy. Around 3 a.m., a bit blitzed, I headed for home. Just as I got in the door, the cuckoo clock in the hall started up and cuckooed 3 times. Quickly realizing my husband would probably wake up, I cuckooed another 9 times. I was really proud of myself for coming up with such a quick-witted solution (even when totally smashed), in order to escape a possible conflict with him. The next morning my husband asked me what time I got in, and I told him midnight. He didn't seem disturbed at all. (Whew! Got away with that one!). Then he said, "We need a new cuckoo clock."

When I asked him why, he said, "Well, last night our clock cuckooed 3 times, then said, "oh, crap," cuckooed 4 more times, cleared its throat, cuckooed another 3 times, giggled, cuckooed twice more, and then tripped over the cat and farted."

One night the husband says to his wife, "Do you want to try a different position tonight? The wife answers: That's a great idea. YOU stand by the sink and do the dishes and I'LL sit on the sofa and fart."

One day a teacher was talking about picking rocks with his Bobcat (tractor). As the teacher continued with the discussion a Blonde was very confused. Finally she raised her hand and said "teacher how did you train your bobcat to pick up rocks."

A married business executive had to make a trip to Palm Beach for his corporation. After a few days, he was enjoying himself so much that he decided to stay another week as part of his vacation.

Wanting to share this newly discovered paradise, he wired his bachelor friend, "Come as soon as you can for a fun week on me. Bring my wife and your mistress."

His friend was quick to wire back, "Your wife and I are arriving tomorrow at 11:30 a.m. How long have you known about us?"

Things NOT to say to the police officer

1. I can't reach my license unless you hold my beer.

2. Sorry, I didn't realize my radar detector wasn't on.

3. Aren't you the guy from the Village People?

4. Hey, you must have been going 125 mph just to keep up with me!

5. I thought you had to be in good physical condition to be a cop.

6. Bad cop! No donut!

7. You're gonna check the trunk, aren't you?

8. I was going to be a cop, really, but I decided to finish high school instead.

9. I pay your salary.

10. That's terrific, the last guy only gave me a warning also.

11. Is that a 9mm? It's nothing compared to this .44 magnum!

12. What do you mean, have I been drinking? You're a trained specialist?

13. Do you know why you pulled me over? Good, at least one of us does.

14. That gut doesn't inspire too much confidence; bet I can outrun you.

15. Didn't I see you get your butt kicked on Cops?

16. Is it true people become cops because they're too dumb to work at McDonald's?

17. I was trying to keep up with traffic.

18. Yes, I know there are no other cars around--That's how far they are ahead of me.

19. Well, when I reached down to pick up my bag of crack, my gun fell off my lap and got lodged between the brake pedal and gas pedal, forcing me to speed out of control.

A young man with an impotency problem consults with a doctor. After several visits and nothing happening the doctor sends him to a hypnotist. The hypnotist puts the young man under and after giving him instructions awakens him. The hypnotist tells him when he says the words; one, two, three, he will have an erection. The young man asks him how to make the erection go down. The hypnotist says just say one, two, three, four and it will subside. There is just one side effect and that is you won't be able to get an erection again for at least ten months. The young guy immediately goes to a bar and picks up a stunning young woman and they proceed to a hotel where he gets the very best suite for $200.00 a night and orders in champagne at $150.00 a bottle. They proceed to get undressed and the excited young man says the magic words "one, two three. "Immediately he has an enormous erection, which the girl admires and asks him "why did you say one, two, three for?"

A man and a little boy entered a barbershop together. After the man received the full treatment - shave, shampoo, manicure, haircut, etc. - he placed the boy in the chair.

"I'm going to buy a green tie to wear for the parade," he said. "I'll be back in a few minutes."

When the boy's haircut was completed and the man still hadn't returned, the barber said, "Looks like your daddy's forgotten all about you." "That wasn't my daddy," said the boy. "He just walked up, took me by the hand and said, 'Come on, son, we're gonna get a free haircut!'"

A man and a woman are sitting next to each other in first class on a plane. The woman sneezes, then takes a tissue and gently wipes it between her legs.

The man isn't sure he saw what she did, and decides he is probably hallucinating. A few minutes pass. The woman sneezes again. She takes a tissue and gently wipes it between her legs.

The man is about to go nuts. He can't believe that he's seeing what he's seeing.

A few more minutes pass. The woman sneezes yet again. She takes a tissue and gently wipes it between her legs yet again.

The man has finally had all he can handle.

He turns to the woman and says, "Three times you've sneezed, and three times you've taken a tissue and wiped it between your legs! What kind of signals are you sending me, or are you just trying to drive me crazy?"

The woman replies, "I am sorry to have disturbed you, sir. I have a rare condition such that when I sneeze, I have an orgasm."

The man, now feeling bad, says, "Oh, I'm sorry. What are you taking for it?"

The woman looks at him and says, "Pepper."

At school one day the teacher heard cat noises coming from the class, and she discovered Little Johnny with a cat under his shirt. She said, "Why have you got your cat at school?"

Little Johnny started crying. "I'm trying to save his life. I woke up this morning to hear the mailman tell my Mommy, 'I'm gonna eat your pussy today!'"

A Chicago lawyer named George successfully defends a major crime lord from charges of dealing drugs, racketeering, murder, kidnapping, and selling arms. As he is leaving the courtroom, an indignant old woman grabs him by the arm. "Young man, where are your Christian scruples?

I believe you would defend Satan himself!"

"I don't know," George says, "what has your kid done?"

A woman went to a pet shop and immediately spotted a large beautiful parrot. There was a sign on the cage that said $50.00.

"Why so little," she asked the pet store owner.

The owner looked at her and said, "Look, I should tell you first that this bird used to live in a house of prostitution, and sometimes it says some pretty vulgar stuff."

The woman thought about this, but decided she had to have the bird anyway. She took it home and hung the bird's cage up in her living room and waited for it to say something. The bird looked around the room, then at her, and said, "New house, new madam." The woman was a bit shocked at the implication, but then thought "that's not so bad."

When her two teenage daughters returned from school the bird saw them and said, "New house, new madam, new whores."

The girls and the woman were a bit offended but then began to laugh about the situation.

Moments later, the woman's husband, Keith, came home from work. The bird looked at him and said, "Hi Keith."

A hillbilly was making his first visit to a hospital where his teenage son was about to have an operation. Watching the doctor's every move, he asked, "What's that?"

The doctor explained, "This is an anesthetic. After he gets this he won't know a thing."

"Save your time, Doc," exclaimed the man. "He don't know shit now."

On his wedding day, the groom walked down the aisle with a big grin on his face. His best man said, "I know this is your wedding day but I've never seen you with such a big smile." The groom whispered, "I just got the best blow job I've ever had."

As the bride walked down the isle she also grinned from ear to ear. Her bridesmaid said to her, "I know this is the happiest day in your life but I have never seen you with a bigger smile."

To which the bride replied, "I've just given my last blow job."

A lawyer was on his deathbed in his bedroom, and he called to his wife. She rushed in and said, "What is it, honey?"

He told her to run and get the bible as soon as possible. Being a religious woman, she thought this was a good idea. She ran and got it, prepared to read him his favorite verse or something of the sort.

He snatched it from her and began quickly scanning pages, his eyes darting right and left. The wife was curious.

"What are you doing, honey?" she asked.

"I'm looking for loopholes!" he shouted.

Prison Pick Up Lines

"Damn, you are sexy in stripes."

"Is that a zip-gun carefully carved out of a piece of discarded metal found on the floor of the prison license-plate manufacturing shop in your pocket, or are you just glad to see me?"

"You know, normally I don't give in the first 30 seconds, but I guess I'm a sucker for sheer muscle mass."

"Nice teeth. They'd look so much better on the floor of my cell."

"Who wants to marry a multiple murderer?"

"I've been watching you from across the yard for awhile now, and I knew if I didn't work up the courage to just walk over here and ask you to be my bitch, I might regret it for the rest of my life."

A little town had a high birth rate that had attracted the attention of the sociologists at the state university. They wrote a grant proposal; got a huge chunk of money; hired a few additional sociologists, an anthropologist, and a family planning and birth control specialist; moved to town; rented offices; set up their computers; got squared away; and began designing their questionnaires and such.

While the staff was busy getting ready for their big research effort, the project director decided to go to the local drugstore for a cup of coffee. He sat down at the counter, ordered his coffee, and while he was drinking it, he told the druggist what his purpose was in town, he then asked him if he had any idea why the birth rate was so high.

"Sure," said the druggist. "Every morning the six o'clock train comes through here and blows for the crossing. It wakes everybody up, and ... well... it's too late to go back to sleep, and it's too early to get up..."

A guy went into a bar and met a nice girl. They have a few drinks and soon wound up at his place, in bed. They're having a great time. She was on top when suddenly she had an epileptic seizure. She was shaking and foaming at the mouth. Our uninformed male thought this was incredible, the best sex he'd ever had. He finished, but she is still shaking and thrashing about with her seizure. He began to get nervous and took her to the emergency room. A nurse asked what the problem was and he replied, "I think her orgasm's stuck!"

Drowsing contentedly after an afternoon of making love in bed, suddenly there's the sound of a the elevator coming up.

Dreamily, the girl whispers, "Oh, oh, quick get moving, that's my husband."

Quick as a flash, Bill jumps out of bed, rushes to the window to see who parked in the visitors lot and suddenly stops dead. "What d'ya mean?" he bellows "I AM your husband!"

One day little Johnny went to school. His teacher said they were going to play a game. She would place an object behind her and describe it. The first person to get it got a piece of candy. First she said, "The object is red and grows on trees." A kid raised his hand and said "an apple" the teacher said correct. Then she said, "The object is flat and comes in different colors" a different kid raises his hand and said it is a notebook! The teacher said correct. Then Johnny said, "ooh! ooh! Can I try?" The teacher said yes. He stood up and put his hand in his pocket. He said "The object is round, hard, and has a head on it." The teacher said "JOHNNY! GO TO THE OFFICE!!" Johnny said, "No it's a quarter!"

A guy walked into the doctor's office for an appointment. "Would you like to tell me your problem?" the pretty receptionist asked. "I'll need the information for the doctor."

"It's rather embarrassing," the guy stammered. "You see, I have a very large and almost constant erection."

"Well, the doctor is very busy today," the receptionist cooed, "but maybe I can squeeze you in."

A guy meets a childhood pal. "What are you doing for yourself these days?"

"I'm a fireman," his old friend replies.

"Yeah? My 15-year-old kid wants to be a fireman," says the guy. "Well," says his friend, "if you want some good advice, you have to install a pole in your house that will go to the basement so your kid can practice, because the hardest thing for a fireman is to jump off into space and catch that pole in the middle of the night."

Ten years later, the two guys happen to meet again.

"Well, did your son become a fireman?"

"No," says the guy, "but I have two daughters who are exotic dancers."

An evangelist was delivering a flaming sermon on vice that shook the rafters of the mission. "Listen to me, all you cigarette suckers," he thundered, "all you pipe suckers, all you bottle suckers -"

Just then a high squeaky voice interjected from the back row, "Don't forget us!"

Young son woke his father up one morning. While the father was getting out of bed, he realized he had a "morning erection".

In an effort to hide it, He dropped down to his hands and knees and pretended to look under bed for something.

His son says, "What you looking for Dad."

Father says, "I thought I saw the cat run under the bed."

His son asks, "What are you gonna do dad, screw it?"

A middle-aged woman decides to have a face-lift for her birthday. She spends $5000 and feels pretty good about the results. On her way home, she stops at a news stand to buy a newspaper. Before leaving she says to the clerk, "I hope you don't mind my asking, but how old do you think I am?" About 32," was the reply. "I'm exactly 47," the woman says happily.

A little while later she goes into McDonald's and ask the counter girl the very same question. She replies, "I guess about 29." The woman replies, "Nope, I'm 47."

Now she's feeling really good about herself. She stops in a Drugstore on her way down the street. She goes up to the counter to get some mints and asks the clerk this burning question. The clerk responds, "Oh, I'd say 30." Again she proudly responds, "I am 47, but thank you."

While waiting for the bus to go home, she asks an old man the same question He replies, "Lady, I'm 78 and my eyesight is going. Although, when I was young, there was a sure way to tell how old a woman was. It sounds very forward, but it requires you to let me put my hands under your bra. Then I can tell you exactly how old you are."

They waited in silence on the empty street until curiosity got the best of her. She finally blurts out, "What the hell, go ahead." He slips both of his hands under her blouse and under her bra and begins to feel around very slowly and carefully. After a couple of minutes he completes one last squeeze of her breasts and removes his hands and says ,"Madam, you are 47."

Stunned and amazed, the woman says, "That was incredible . . how did you know?"

The old man replies, "I was behind you in line at McDonald's."

"It's really amazing," Ruth told her wealthy middle-aged lover as he was reclining on the bed. "You have a beautiful head of gray hair, but not a single one in your pubic area."

"Not as amazing as you might think," he continued, "my brain has to do all the worrying. "Mr Happy" hasn't got a care in the world."

A young lad was out with his dad in the park when he spotted a woman about to breastfeed her baby. She unbuttoned her blouse, rolled out a very large breast and popped the rosy nipple into the child's mouth.

"Dad! What's that woman doing to that baby?" the lad asked.

"Relax, son. She's just feeding him," the father replied. "Get the fuck outta here!" the boy, exclaimed. "There's no way he'll eat all of that!"

A scientist in Australia has invented a bra which offers more support and prevents a woman's breasts from bouncing up and down. After announcing his invention, the scientist was taken outside and beaten up by a large group of men.

Two rednecks went to a gas station that was holding a contest: A Chance to Win Free Sex when you filled your tank. They pumped their gas and went to pay the attendant who said, "I'm thinking of a number between 1 and 10, if you guess right you win free sex."

"Okay," agreed one of the rednecks, "I guess seven."

"Sorry, I was thinking eight." replied the attendant.

The next week they tried again. When they went to pay, the attendant told them to pick a number.

"Two!" said the second redneck.

"Sorry, it's three," said the attendant, "come back and try again."

As they walked out to their car, one redneck said to the other, "I think this contest is rigged."

"No way," said his buddy,

"My wife won twice last week."

An old nun who was living in a convent next to a Brooklyn construction site noticed the coarse language of the workers and decided to spend some time with them to correct their ways.

She decided she would take her lunch sit with the workers and talk with them. She put her sandwich in a brown bag and walked over to the spot where the men were eating. She walked up to the group and with a big smile said : . . . "Do you men know Jesus Christ?"

They shook their heads and looked at each other. One of the workers looked up into the steelwork and yelled "Anybody up there know Jesus Christ?"

One of the steelworkers asked why.

The worker yelled "His wife is here with his lunch".

Two mothers were talking about their sons. The first said, "My son is such a saint. He works hard, doesn't smoke, and he hasn't so much as looked at a woman in over two years."

The other woman said, "Well, my son is a saint himself. Not only hasn't he not looked at a woman in over three years, but he hasn't touched a drop of liquor in all that time."

"My word," the first mother said. "You must be so proud."

"I am," the second mother replied. "And when he's paroled next month, I'm going to throw him a big party."

An elderly woman went to see her doctor about a small problem. She let farts in church let farts at work, let farts at home, but they didn't smell and you couldn't hear them. So the doctor told her to take this bottle of pills and come back and see him in a week. She came back a week later mad as hell. Doc those pills you gave me made my farts smell terrible. Doctor told her now that I have your sinus cleared up we well work on your hearing next.

At the end of the night a man leaves the bar.

Outside he sees a nun. He walks over to her and slaps her in the face. Then he punches her in the stomach and knocks her over. He proceeds to kick her several times and when he's done he bends down to her and says, "not so tough tonight, are you Batman?"

A fellow is getting ready to tee-off on the first hole when a second fellow approaches and asks if he can join him. The first says that he usually plays alone but agrees to let the second guy join him.

Both are even after the first couple of holes. The second guy says, "Say, we're about evenly matched, how about we play for five bucks a hole?"

The first fellow says that he usually plays alone and doesn't like to bet but agrees to the terms. Well, the second guy wins the rest of the holes and as they're walking off of the eighteenth hole, and while counting his $80.00, he confesses that he's the pro at a neighboring course and likes to pick on suckers.

The first fellow reveals that he's the Parish Priest at the local Catholic Church to which the second fellow gets all flustered and apologetic and offers to give the Priest back his money. The Priest says, "No, no. You won fair and square and I was foolish to bet with you. You keep your winnings."

The pro says, "Well, is there anything I can do to make it up to you?"

The Priest says, "Well, you could come to Mass on Sunday and make a donation. Then, if you bring your mother and father by after Mass, I'll marry them for you."

A West Virginia teeny bopper comes home from school and asks, "Ma, is it true that babies come out of the place boys put their wieners in?"

Ma replies ,"Yep, sho' do."

Daughter says," Why Ma, is that why you are missin yo' front teeth?"

The New York Police Department were investigating the mysterious death of a prominent businessman who had jumped from a window of his 11th-story office. Jill, his voluptuous private secretary could offer no explanation for the action but said that her boss had been acting peculiarly ever since she started working for him, a month ago. "After my very first week on the job," Jill said, "I received a $20 raise. At the end of the 2nd week he called me into his private office, gave me a lovely black nightie, five pairs of nylon stockings and said, 'These are for a beautiful efficient secretary."

"At the end of the third week he gave me a fabulous mink. Then, this afternoon, he called me into his private office again, presented me with this fabulous diamond bracelet and asked me if I could consider making love to him and what it would cost."

"I told him that I would, and because he had been so nice to me, he could have it for $5, although I was charging all the other guys in the office ten. That's when he jumped out the window."

Wife coming down the stairs ask her husband lying on a sofa what he has been doing.

He replied, 'Killing Flies'.

She said, 'How many you have killed so far ?'

He, 'Five, three males and two females'

She, 'How did you figure that out ?'

He, 'Three were sitting on the Remote and Two were sitting on the phone'.

A policeman was interrogating three blondes who were training to become detectives. To test their skills in recognizing a suspect, he shows the first blonde a picture for five seconds and then hides it.

"This is your suspect, how would you recognize him?"

The first blonde answers: "That's easy, we'll catch him fast because he only has one eye!"

The policeman says, "Well...uh...he has one eye because the picture shows his PROFILE, a SIDE VIEW. That's just ONE SIDE of him!"

Slightly flustered by this ridiculous response, he flashes the picture for five seconds at the second blonde and asks her:

"This is your suspect, how would you recognize him?" The second blonde giggles, flips her hair and says: "Ha! He'd be too easy to catch because he only has one ear!"

The policeman angrily responds: "What's the matter with you two? Of course only one eye and one ear are SHOWING because it's a picture of his profile! Is that the best answer you can come up with?!"

Extremely frustrated at this point, he shows the picture to the third blonde and in a very testy voice asks: "This is your suspect, how would you recognize him?"

The blonde looks at the picture intently for a moment and says: "Hmmmm... the suspect wears contact lenses."

The policeman is surprised and speechless because he really doesn't know himself if the suspect wears contacts or not. "Well, that's an interesting answer! Wait here for a few minutes while I check his file, and I'll get back to you on that."

He leaves the room and goes to his office, checks the suspect's file in his computer and comes back with a beaming smile on his face.

"Wow! I can't believe it... it's TRUE! The suspect does in fact wear contact lenses. Good work! How were you able to make such an astute observation?"

"That's easy," the blonde replied.

"He can't wear regular glasses, because he only has one eye and one ear!"

A man and his wife were having some problems at home and were giving each other the silent treatment. The next week, the man realized that he would need his wife to wake him at 5:00 AM for an early morning business flight to Chicago. Not wanting to be the first to break the silence (AND LOSE), he wrote on a piece of paper, "Please wake me at 5:00 AM.

The next morning the man woke up, only to discover it was 9:00 AM and that he had missed his flight. Furious, he was about to go and see why his wife hadn't woken him when he noticed a piece of paper by the bed.

The paper said, "It is 5:00 AM. Wake up."

(MEN JUST AREN'T EQUIPPED FOR THESE SORT OF CONTESTS)

Little Johnny, Billy and Tommy were walking home from school one warm spring day. As they were cutting through the alleys and backyards, they happened to look through a hole in the fence of one of the yards where a woman was sunbathing in the nude.

As they looked through the hole, Johnny suddenly started to scream, left his friends and took off running for home.

The next day, as the three boys came home again, they found the same hole in the fence and started to watch the woman. Again, after just a few minutes, Johnny started screaming and ran off quickly.

On the third day, the boys were peeping into the hole in the fence again after school, when Johnny turned around and started to run again.

But this time, Bill and Tommy grabbed him and demanded to know what was wrong.

Johnny replied, "My mother told me that if I ever looked at a naked woman, I would turn to stone...."

"And I started to feel a part of me getting awfully hard........"

A guy comes walking into a bar with a turtle in his hand. The turtle's one eye is black and blue, two of his legs are bandaged, and his whole shell is taped together with duct tape. The bartender looks at the guy and asks:

"What's wrong with your turtle?"

"Not a thing," the man responds, this beat up turtle is faster than your dog!"

"Not a chance!", replies the barkeep.

"Okay then, says the guy... you take your dog and let him stand at one end of the bar.

Then go and stand at the other end of the room and call your dog. I'll bet you $500 that before your dog reaches you, my turtle will be there."

So the bartender, thinking it's an easy $500, agrees. The bartender goes to the other side of the bar, and on the count of three calls his dog.

Suddenly the guy picks up his turtle and throws it across the room, narrowly missing the bartender, and smashing into the wall and says - "I WIN... Told you it'll be there before your dog!"

A woman gives birth to a baby, and afterwards, the doctor comes in, and he says, "I have to tell you something about your baby."

The woman sits up in bed and says, "What's wrong with my baby, Doctor?

What's wrong???"

The doctor says, "It's ok, nothing's wrong, exactly, but your baby is a little bit different. Your baby is a hermaphrodite."

The woman says, "A hermaphrodite...what's that?"

The doctor says, "Well, it means your baby has the ...er... features ...of a both a male and a female."

The woman turns pale. She says, "Oh my god!

You mean it has a penis...AND a brain?"

Kelly meets up with her blonde friend June as she's picking up her car from the mechanic. Kelly asks, "Everything ok with your car now?"

"Yes, thank goodness," June replies.

"Weren't you worried that the mechanic might try to rip you off?"

"Yeah, but he didn't. I was SO relieved when he handed me a bill for only $42. He told me all I needed was blinker fluid!"

An old lady was lying on her deathbed and her husband was sitting by her side when the wife turned to her husband and said, "I have to tell you something. In my table drawer is a black box. Look in it, come back and tell me what you see."

So the husband went home and looked in the box and found 50,000 dollars and 3 eggs. The next day the husband went back to his wife and said he had found 50,000 dollars and 3 eggs, and then he asked what the money and eggs where for.

The wife replied, "Each time we made love and I was disappointed I put 1 egg in the box."

The husband smiled because there were only 3 eggs in the box, but his wife quickly noticed the smile and said, "Every time I collected 1 dozen eggs I would sell them in the market and put the money in the black box."

A guy is at the pearly gates, waiting to be admitted, while St. Peter is leafing through the big book to see if the guy is worthy of entering. Saint Peter goes through the book several times, furrows his brow, and says to the guy, "You know, I can't see that you did anything really good in your life, but, you never did anything bad either. Tell you what, if you can tell me of one REALLY good deed that you did in your life, you're in."

The guy thinks for a moment and says, "Well, there was the time when I was driving down the highway and I saw a group of biker guys gathered around this poor girl. I slowed down my car to see what was going on, and sure enough, there were about 20 of 'em tormenting this girl."

"Infuriated, I got out my car, grabbed a tire iron out of my trunk, and walked straight up to the leader of the gang, a huge guy with a studded leather jacket and a chain running from his nose to his ear. As I walked up to the leader, the gang formed a circle around me. So, I ripped the leader's chain off his face and smashed him over the head with the tire iron. Then I turned around and yelled to the rest of them, 'Leave this poor, innocent girl alone! You're all a bunch of sick, deranged animals!

Go home before I teach you all a lesson in pain!'"

St. Peter, impressed, says, "Really? When did this happen?"

"Oh, about two minutes ago."

Hilary is not feeling well. She goes to her doctor and gets a complete physical, only to find out that she is pregnant. She is furious and can't believe this has happened. She calls the White House and gets Bill on the phone, and immediately begins to berate him, screaming: "How could you have let this happen? With all of the trouble going on right now, you go and get me pregnant!!! How could you?!

I just found out I am pregnant and it is your fault! How could you??? What have you got to say???"

There is nothing but silence on the phone. She screams again: "CAN YOU HEAR ME???

Bill's quiet voice comes on in a barely audible whisper..."Who is this?"

For my fiftieth birthday this year, my husband (the dear) purchased a week of personal training at the local health club for me. Although I am still in great shape since playing on my high school softball team, I decided it would be a good idea to go ahead and give it a try. I called the club and made my reservations with a personal trainer I'll call Bruce, who identified himself as a 26 year old aerobics instructor and model for athletic clothing and swim wear. My husband seemed pleased with my enthusiasm to get started. The club encouraged me to keep a diary to chart my progress.

Monday:

Started my day at 6:00am. Tough to get out of bed, but found it was well worth it when I arrived at the health club to find Bruce waiting for me. He is something of a Greek God - with blond hair, dancing eyes and a dazzling white smile. Woo Hoo!! Bruce gave me a tour and showed me the machines. He took my pulse after five minutes on the treadmill. He was alarmed that my pulse was so fast, but I attribute it to standing next to him in his Lycra aerobic outfit. I enjoyed watching the skillful way in which he conducted his aerobics class after my workout today. Very inspiring. Bruce was encouraging as I did my sit-ups, although my gut was already aching from holding it in the whole time he was around. This is going to be a FANTASTIC week!!

Tuesday:

I drank a whole pot of coffee, but I finally made it out the door. Bruce made me lie on my back and push a heavy iron bar into the air - then he put weights on it! My legs were a little wobbly on the treadmill, but I made the full mile. Bruce's rewarding smile made it all worthwhile. I feel GREAT!! It's a whole new life for me.

Wednesday:

The only way I can brush my teeth is by laying on the toothbrush on the counter and moving my mouth back and forth over it. I believe I have a hernia in both pectorals. Driving was OK as long as I didn't try to steer or stop. I parked on top of a GEO in the club parking lot. Bruce was impatient with me, insisting that my screams bothered other club members His voice is a little too perky for early in the morning and when he scolds, he gets this nasally whine that is VERY annoying. My chest hurt when I got on the treadmill, so Bruce put me on the stair monster. Why the hell would anyone invent a machine to simulate an activity rendered obsolete by elevators? Bruce told me it would help me get in shape and enjoy life.

He said some other shit too.

Thursday:

Bruce was waiting for me with his vampire-like teeth exposed as his thin, cruel lips were pulled back in a full snarl. I couldn't help being a half an hour late, it took me that long to tie my shoes. Bruce took me to work out with dumbbells. When he was not looking, I ran and hid in the men's room. He sent Lars to find me, then, as punishment, put me on the rowing machine - which I sank.

Friday:

I hate that bastard Bruce more than any human being has ever hated any other human being in the history of the world. Stupid, skinny, anemic little cheerleader. If there was a part of my body I could move without unbearable pain, I would beat him with it. Bruce wanted me to work on my triceps. I don't have any triceps! And if you don't want dents in the floor, don't hand me the &*@*#$ barbells or anything that weighs more than a sandwich. (Which I am sure you learned in the sadist school you attended and graduated magna cum laude from.) The treadmill flung me off and I landed on a health and nutrition teacher. Why couldn't it have been someone softer, like the drama coach or the choir director?

Saturday:

Bruce left a message on my answering machine in his grating, shrilly voice wondering why I did not show up today. Just hearing him made me want to smash the machine with my planner. However, I lacked the strength to even use the TV remote and ended up catching eleven straight hours of the *$@#&& Weather Channel.

Sunday:

I'm having the Church van pick me up for services today so I can go and thank GOD that this week is over. I will also pray that next year my husband (the BASTARD) will choose a gift for me that is fun.

Two boys were playing football in Golden Gate Park when one is attacked by a Rottweiler. Thinking quickly, the other boy rips off a board of the nearby fence, wedges it down the dog's collar & twists, breaking the dog's neck. A reporter who was walking by sees the incident, and rushes over to interview the boy!

"Forty Niners' fan saves friend from vicious animal," he starts writing in his notebook.

"But I'm not a Niners' fan," the boy replied.

"Oakland Raiders' fan rescues friend from horrific attack," the reporter starts again.

"I'm not a Raiders' fan either," the boy said.

"Then what are you?" the reporter asked.

"I'm a Cowboys' fan."

The reporter turns to a new sheet in his notebook and writes, "Redneck bastard kills family pet."

The old Cherokee chief sat in his reservation hut smoking the ceremonial pipe and eyeing the two US government officials sent to interview him. "Chief Two Eagles," one official began, "you have observed the white man for many generations, you have seen his wars and his products, you have seen all his progress and all his problems."

The chief nodded.

The official continued, "Considering recent events, in your opinion where has the white man gone wrong?"

The chief stared at the government officials for over a minute, and then calmly replied:

"When white man found this land Indians were running it. No taxes. No debt. Plenty buffalo. Plenty beaver. Women did most of the work. Medicine man free. Indian men hunted and fished all the time."

The chief smiled and added quietly, "White man dumb enough to think he could improve system like that."

A guy waiting at the bus stop wearing chains, leather jaket, and leather pants and his hair in long spikes each a different color. An old man at the bus stop looked and looked at the guy, finally, the guy said to the old man: "haven't you ever done anything crazy and wild in your life" and the old man said "yah, I have, I once made it with a peacock and I was wondering if your my son"

The Herbert's were unable to conceive children, and decided to use a surrogate father to start their family.

On the day the proxy father was to arrive, Mr. Herbert kissed his wife and said, "I'm off. The man should be here soon". Half an hour later, just by chance, a door-to-door baby photographer rang the doorbell, hoping to make a sale.

"Good morning madam. I've come to...." "Oh, no need to explain. Come in," Mrs. Herbert cut in. "Really?" the photographer asked. "Well, good! My specialty is babies."

"That's what my husband and I had hoped. Please come in and have a seat."

After a moment she asked, blushing, "Well, where do we start?"

Photographer - "Leave everything to me. I usually try two in the bathtub, one on the couch and perhaps a couple on the bed. Sometimes the living room floor is fun too. You can really spread out!"

Wife - "Bathtub, couch, bed, living room floor? No wonder it didn't work for my husband and me."

Photographer - "Well, madam, none of us can guarantee a good one every time."

But if we try several different positions and I shoot from six or seven angles, I'm sure you'll be pleased with the results."

Wife - "My, my, that's a lot of...."

Photographer - "Madam, in my line of work, a man must take his time. I'd love to be in and out in five minutes, but you'd be disappointed with that, I'm sure."

Wife (muttering)- "Don't I know it."

The photographer opened his briefcase and pulled out a portfolio of his baby pictures. "This was done on the top of a bus."

Wife - "Oh my!"

Photographer - "And these twins turned out exceptionally well, when you consider their mother was so difficult to work with."

Wife - "She was difficult?"

Photographer - "Yes, I'm afraid so. I finally had to take her to the park to get the job done right. People were crowding around four and five deep, pushing to get a good look."

Wife - "Four and five deep?" (Eyes wide).

Photographer - "Yes, and for more than three hours, too. The mother was constantly squealing and yelling - I could hardly concentrate! Then darkness approached and I began to rush my shots. Finally, when the squirrels began nibbling on my equipment, I just packed it all in."

Wife (leaning forward) - "You mean they actually chewed on your ....equipment?"

Photographer - "That's right. Well, madam, if you're ready, I'll set up my tripod so that we can get to work"

Wife - "Tripod?"

Photographer - "Oh yes, I have to use a tripod to rest my Canon on. It's much too big for me to hold very long. Madam? Madam? Good heavens, she's fainted!"

Jack was arrested for selling home-stilled whiskey. His lawyer put him on the stand and asked the jurors to look carefully at his client.

"Now, Ladies and Gentleman of the jury," concluded the lawyer, "you've looked carefully at the defendant.

Can you sit there in the jury and honestly believe that if my client had a quart of whiskey he would sell it?"

He was acquitted.

Some "dirtbag" in Polk County Florida who got pulled over in a routine traffic stop ended up "executing" the deputy who stopped him. The deputy was shot eight times, including once behind his right ear at close range. Another deputy was wounded and a police dog killed. A statewide manhunt ensued.

The low-life was found hiding in a wooded area with his gun. SWAT team officers fired and hit the guy 68 times. Now here's the kicker:

Naturally, the media asked why they shot him 68 times.

Polk County Sheriff Grady Judd, told the Orlando Sentinel:

"That's all the bullets we had!"

(Talk about an all time classic answer!!!)

In a murder trial, the defense attorney was cross-examining a pathologist. Here's what happened:

Attorney: Before you signed the death certificate, had you taken the pulse? Coroner: No.

Attorney: Did you listen to the heart? Coroner: No.

Attorney: Did you check for breathing? Coroner: No.

Attorney: So, when you signed the death certificate, you weren't sure the man was dead, were you? Coroner: Well, let me put it this way. The man's brain was sitting in a jar on my desk. But I guess it's possible he could be out there practicing law somewhere.

When things in your life seem almost too much to handle, when 24 hours in a day are not enough, remember the mayonnaise jar and the beer.

A professor stood before his philosophy class and had some items in front of him. When the class began, wordlessly, he picked up a very large and empty mayonnaise jar and proceeded to fill it with golf balls. He then asked the students if the jar was full. They agreed that it was.

So the professor then picked up a box of pebbles and poured them into the jar. He shook the jar lightly. The pebbles rolled into the open areas between the golf balls. He then asked the students again if the jar was full. They agreed it was.

The professor next picked up a box of sand and poured it into the jar.

Of course, the sand filled up everything else. He asked once more if the jar was full. The students responded with a unanimous "yes."

The professor then produced two cans of beer from under the table and poured the entire contents into the jar, effectively filling the empty space between the sand. The students laughed.

Now," said the professor, as the laughter subsided, "I want you to recognize that this jar represents your life. The golf balls are the important things--your family, your children, your health, your friends, your favorite passions--things that if everything else was lost and only they remained, your life would still be full. "The pebbles are the other things that matter like your job, your house, your car. The sand is everything else-- the small stuff. If you put the sand into the jar first," he continued, there is no room for the pebbles or the golf balls. The same goes for life.

If you spend all your time and energy on the small stuff, you will never have room for the things that are important to you. Pay attention to the things that are critical to your happiness. Play with your children. Take time to get medical checkups. Take your partner out to dinner. Play another 18.

There will always be time to clean the house, and fix the disposal.

"Take care of the golf balls first, the things that really matter. Set your priorities. The rest is just sand."

One of the students raised her hand and inquired what the beer represented.

The professor smiled. "I'm glad you asked. It just goes to show you that no matter how full your life may seem, there's always room for a couple of beers."

About the Author:

Tom was born in Washington DC on November 14, 1956. The eldest son of Thomas and Margaret Hatchett. He and his 3 sisters would live in different states as many Air Force Families have until his father's retirement in 1971. At that time the family settled down in Danville Virginia. Tom graduated from Chatham High School in 1975 and went to work at the local Goodyear Tire and Rubber Co. Prior to this he married for the first time. They were blessed with a beautiful blond haired daughter they named Misty in 1981. Unfortunately they decided that they wanted to go their separate ways in 1982. A few years later Tom decided to try it again. Although the marriage went sour fast, the byproduct was 2 more little blue-eyed blond haired beauties named Molly and Tiffany. Hopefully the third time is the charm and this third marriage will be the last. I know I have to keep this wife, because when I asked my father-in-law for his blessings he looked me straight in the eye and said " I've done give her away twice already, I'm not taking her back anymore." I started in Law Enforcement with the prison system in the mid 80s. A lot of people figured I would end up in prison anyway, so I figured I might as well go ahead and join now, rather than being forced to go in later. Faced with raising kids and stepchildren Tom ended up working full time and part-time jobs in this field. He worked as a correctional officer, a juvenile detention officer, a deputy sheriff, outreach detention counselor, home electronic monitoring officer, a law enforcement trainer and several more jobs. One thing that he tried to maintain during all of this was a sense of humor. With what the good folks in law enforcement are paid, you have to have a sense of humor. Tom had an Aunt who was always swapping jokes with him and she told him one day that she wished she had written all the jokes down she had heard and put them in a book, because she could sell it and make a million dollars. Well for 23 years I wrote the jokes down and finally since I retired the joke book is getting published. I figure I probably have a better chance of making a million off the lottery than my writing, but if this book brings a smile and a chuckle to you and in any way makes your day better. I'll be happy. Thanks so much for reading my book and I sincerely hope you enjoy it.

Printed in Great Britain
by Amazon

71495286R00106